The Intrepid Fox
In the Paddle River Valley

By
Helen Liss Ivanhoe Smart

August, 2007

To Chuck and Shirley,
     I count myself
fortunate to have two
such loyal and true
friends.
     Good luck always.
               Helen

Helen Liss Ivanhoe Smart

Heritage Books Canada
Copyright © 2006 by Helen Liss Ivanhoe Smart
First published by Heritage Books Canada in softcover in 2006
Published in Canada by Heritage Books Canada,
#374, 9768-170 Street, Edmonton, Alberta, Canada, T5T 5L4

www.heritagebookscanada.com

Note for Librarians: A cataloguing record for this book is available from Library and Archives Canada at www.collectionscanada.ca/amicus/index-e.html

Library and Archives Canada Cataloguing in Publication
Smart, Helen
The Intrepid Fox / Helen Smart
Summary: The life story of the author's father and his exploits and achievements as an early western Canadian immigrant settler.

First published: Edmonton, Alberta, Canada : Heritage Books Canada, 2006
World-wide Distribution: Victoria, B.C; Toronto, Canada; London, England; Melbourne, Australia; New York, N.Y.

ISBN 978-1-4251-0431-3

I. Liss, John, 1892-1986 --- historical non-fiction
Printed in Canada

U.S. Publisher Cataloging-in-Publication Data (Library of Congress Standards)
Smart, Helen
The Intrepid Fox / by Helen Smart
Originally first published by Heritage Books Canada, Edmonton, Alberta, Canada, 2006
Heritage Books Canada acknowledges with thanks the various organizations and societies that support work of this author and our publishing program.
Layout and Design by: Reuben Bauer
Cover Image and Design: Eye Captured Images
Text photo images: Photosbyrubens
Book Developer: Reuben Bauer

Order online at:
trafford.com/06-2188

10 9 8 7 6 5

Table of Contents

My Paddle Valley Home

The Liss Homestead

Home! Home is where the heart is and part of my heart will always remain in the beautiful Paddle River Valley and the house where I was born. There were seven of us Liss kids, five boys and two girls, children of Polish immigrant pioneers who settled on virgin land northwest of Edmonton, Alberta near a place called Sangudo. When our father, John Liss, homesteaded on 160 acres in 1916, only native Chippewa Indians had been there before him. Poplar, spruce and tamarack covered the hills and lush grasses grew in the flatlands of the Paddle River Valley. "The Flats," we called this 2-mile wide meadow, home to wildlife and native flowers and berries in lush profusion. Far to the north, beyond the river, across our valley we could see the distant blue hills of places called Roydale and Peavine – another world, too far away to visit.

We were pioneers, a hardworking closely knit family growing up in a sparsely-settled countryside with few roads, no electricity, no phone, no running water, a wood stove, no indoor plumbing and only an outdoor privy. But we had devoted parents who gave us support, encouragement and a feeling of self-worth. We were a unit working together. Each of us seven children knew we had a chore to do that was essential to the family's survival.

When I left my home in 1949 to begin married life in distant California, I thought I was leaving the most beautiful place in the whole world. A long driveway flanked by towering Colorado Blue Spruce led past a hawthorn hedge to a circular drive in front of our two-story white house. Tall birches grew on either side of the wide front porch. A green lawn spongy with years of grass clippings framed mother's colorful flower garden along the south side of the house. It was a welcoming place where I always felt at peace.

This is the story of my parents John and Mary Liss, and of their children Stanley, Vlad, Helen, Edward, Ted, Valeria and John Robert and of their successes and sorrows during those pioneer days of the 1920's and 1930's in northwestern Alberta.

John Boleslaus Pozarzyski

John Liss

John Boleslaus Pozarzyski was born July 10, 1892 in Hlevin near Borisov, Russia. In 1903 his father immigrated to America to escape being conscripted to work on the Trans Siberian railroad. In 1904 when John was listed on the ship's manifest as 10 years old, the rest of the Pozarzyski family joined their father in Baltimore, Maryland. After a 14-day trip in steerage, the mother and 8 children arrived in America with $40.00 cash. Young John said as the S.S. Chemnetz approached Baltimore harbor, he was amazed to see so many tall buildings, all so close together. As the steamship drew closer in he saw huge pictures of a man hanging in all directions from the buildings and on the walls. What was this all about? Who was this man, the young lad wondered. He'd never seen anything like this back in Russia. Later he learned that 1904 was a presidential election year and that the man in those photos was Teddy Roosevelt who was running for re-election.

The elder Pozarzyski settled his wife and eight children in Toledo, Ohio but those early days were very difficult for the newly arrived immigrant family. There was little money, crowded living conditions and a resentment against Polish newcomers. One day the children were all taken from their mother because the authorities said they were starving. Not until the intervention of the Catholic priest were her children returned to Mrs. Pozarzyski.

On the streets of Toledo, John witnessed an act that was reprehensible to him. A man in a buggy regularly traveled the streets, passing out cigarettes and chewing tobacco to the young children playing in the streets.

"Making addicts out of innocents. Tobacco companies interested in that God Almighty Dollar. They have no conscience. It was a great injustice." He was opposed to tobacco all his life.

John's father would leave his wife and children for long periods, searching for work. John wanted to attend school, but his mother needed help in feeding her children, six of them younger than John, so John took any job he could find for meager sums, every bit helped. He saw an ad for work at the Canadian National Exposition in Toronto, Canada and decided to apply. That visit changed his life. He learned that in Western Canada a settler could obtain 160 acres for a $10 filing fee. All that land for only $10.00 – he dreamed of becoming a land-owner.

In 1911, at 19 years of age, John began his ambitious land search across Western Canada, driven by a burning desire to become a farmer. He traveled across Alberta, into British Columbia, then back to Alberta. The vastness and richness of this virgin country, inspired him with en-thusiasm, so much so that he persuaded his father to leave the U.S. and join him in Calgary where the two men opened a Polish book store.

John left his father to run the store and he pursued his dreams, tramping across Northern Alberta, pack on his back, undaunted by daily hardships. Once he nearly drowned in the Smoky River when he was caught in a whirlpool; only the heroic efforts of his strong swim-ming companion saved him. Another time he missed a scheduled river boat on the Athabasca River and decided to make a raft and float downstream to his destination, but the raft was wrecked on a rock and he ended up walking 40 miles to Athabasca Landing. One night he ate dried muskrat meat with an Indian family, a welcome meal to a tired, hungry man.

At last in the Peace River Country of Northern Alberta, he found a beautiful spot. He filed on a ¼ section, only to realize later that this area was too remote, too far from a railroad. He gave up the land and lost his $10.00 filing fee.

Luck was not with the young new homesteader. The economy of Canada became stagnant. High unemployment and a looming depres-sion forced him to try for job opportunities in the U.S. Things were no better there, hundreds of men trudged from establishment to estab-lishment hoping for work.

Our father told us that in those "hard time days" he worked at any job he could find – as a lumberjack, a sawmill hand, newspaper agent, printer, clothing salesman, life insurance salesman, teamster, nurseryman, copper miner and real estate salesman. His shortest term of employment was ½ day in a tunnel in Seattle. When he saw two men killed in front of him, he said, "I'm out of here!"

What was John to do? He had no money and no job. He saw a sign, "Join the U.S. Marines. Get a free education." At last he might have a chance to get the education he always craved. In 1913, John joined the U.S. Marines. He was deployed on a warship and sent to Mazatlan where the Marines awaited orders from Washington to invade Mexico.

When he returned to Marine headquarters at Mare Island, California, he decided to change his name to a simpler spelling. Anglo-Saxons had great difficulty with a name like Pozarzyski.

"How do you spell that funny name?" they would ask.

John decided to pick a short name with a connotation. He picked "Liss" which in Polish means "fox."

"How do you spell "Liss?" people would ask.

"I should have left my name Pozarzyski," he would say in disgust.

His term in the Marines was brief. The promise of a free education never materialized and because his mother needed him for support he was able, by purchase, to receive an honorable discharge. When WW I broke out shortly after his discharge, he was in Los Angles in front of the Times Building organizing a march on Washington to demand work. Sometimes he wondered if he would ever get ahead. Would these hard times last forever?

It was 1916 when the restless young John Liss made a decision. He would return to Canada and make it his permanent home. Together he and his father decided to homestead on land in the beautiful Paddle River Valley. Before long, they had erected a small log cabin on Grandfather's portion.

Grandfather's ¼ section was SW 19-57-6 the southwest quarter of section 19, township 57, range 6. Our Dad's homestead was SE 24-57-7, the southeast quarter of section 24, township 57, range 7. The two parcels were ½ mile apart, both on fertile land, with ample timber and meadows of grass.

They sent for Grandmother Pozarzyski to join them. She left New York where she had been living with a daughter and came "Out West" but she hated the pioneer life and husband and wife quarreled constantly. Within a short time, Grandmother left the cabin and went to work in the Sangudo Hotel.

"Mother disgraced Father and me," my dad told me in later years. "I did not want to have anything to do with her." He did not speak of his mother. He did not correspond with her. We children did not know she existed.

Grandmother and Grandfather Pozarzyski never got along. The

story we kids were told is that back in Poland, Grandmother as a very young woman, had been betrothed to Grandfather, a much older man. But he didn't want to wait for his betrothed to come of age so he married another woman, closer to his age. When that woman unexpectedly died, Grandfather proceeded to claim his betrothed, his legitimate right. Grandmother, meantime, had fallen in love and run off with a Cossack and forever resented that she had been "torn from the arms of her lover." When John's family came to America, his parents often lived apart.

John was eager to "prove-up" his homestead, but he knew his patriotic duty was to enter the military to protect his new homeland. He left Grandfather Pozarzyski in charge of things and joined the Canadian Army.

In 1917 while he was stationed in Ontario, he met and married an Irish Canadian girl, Bernice Blanche Rynard. Their son, Kenneth Rademir Liss was born March 15, 1919. After his discharge from the Army, John eagerly returned to his homestead to prepare a home for his wife and son's arrival. Blanche and the baby remained in Udora, Ontario with her family.

When Bernice and Kenneth arrived in Sangudo our Dad had not yet completed a house on his own land and the young couple had to move in with Grandfather Pozarzyski in his little 12' x 12' cabin. Dad could tell Bernice was disappointed. What woman wouldn't be? She had left a civilized older area of Canada to come to a primitive lonely land with no roads, no telephones, no electricity, few neighbors and never-ending work. I have seen her letters from 1919 to her family in Udora – no complaints but poignant comments on how much she missed them. She loved her baby boy, Kenneth. She wrote, "My little lad is the picture of health, golden hair, fat cheeks and long black lashes. I had to get a bigger box for him because he kicked himself out of the old one. He plays for hours with his toys, two round tins with lids."

Suddenly, in the spring of 1920, Bernice became ill and died. She died of tubercular spinal meningitis leaving behind a widower and a 1½ year old son.

Bernice Liss is buried in Beachmont Cemetery in Edmonton.

Grandfather Pozarzyski's 12′ x 12′ cabin. Home to Grandfather, John, Bernice and Kenneth Liss – 1918.

Dad and Grandfather tried to take care of Kenneth but the ever-pressing task of clearing the land and the task of feeding and clothing the baby was overwhelming.

John sent for his 16 year old sister Josephine to come from Eastern Canada to help but shortly after her arrival a handsome young man from Greencourt, 20 miles away came courting. It was love at first sight and soon the young Louis Mycon had married and spirited Josephine away.

Bernice's family in Udora begged John Liss to send Kenneth to them, but John wanted to keep his son with him. Sometimes when he and Grandfather went to work in the fields, they left Kenneth in the yard, a stake pounded into the ground and the boy tied to the stake with a rope around his waist. Neighbors were sympathetic and would stop on their way to market to check on "that poor Liss baby." Our Dad said it broke his heart to come in from the field and find his son with wet diapers and mud on his face. There was no one to hire to take care of the child; all the settlers had their own problems of survival. John reluctantly decided Kenneth would be better off with his mother's family in Udora because he could not properly care for his son on the farm.

A lady from Sangudo, Mrs. Neil McIvor, was going by train to Toronto and she agreed to take Kenneth with her. Bernice's family met them in Toronto and took Kenneth to their home in Udora. John Liss did not see his son again until 1942 when both men were in the military and met in Calgary, Alberta.

Dad said one of the sorrows of his life was that he had been unable to raise his own son. During all these ensuing hard times there had never been enough money for the train fare to bring Kenneth back to Sangudo. John would never have given up his boy if he could have foreseen how soon he would remarry.

John Liss grieved for the death of his wife and the loss of his young son. He and his father spent the summer working long hours clearing huge trees from the virgin land, stopping to do all the pressing farm chores only when darkness came. Finally all the animals watered and fed, two weary men sat down to prepare a meal for themselves. John knew he could not succeed as a farmer without a wife and helpmate, but he knew of no unattached young women in the Sangudo area. Perhaps if he could talk to someone who traveled extensively around northwestern Alberta, that person might know of a single young woman.

But where to find such a person? Of course! There was indeed such a person – the man from the Soldier Settlement Board.

After World War I the Canadian government gave a grant of land to the veterans "for services rendered." John was able to get a soldier's grant of 160 acres adjoining his homestead. A Soldier Settlement Board was created to assist the veterans. An agent of that Board traveled this area of Alberta visiting the veterans and offering advice and guidance to the novice farmers. John looked forward to the agent's next visit.

When the Soldier Settlement Board agent came by in the fall, John asked him if in all his travels he had met any young woman of marriageable age.

The S.S.B. man thought for a moment. "Yes," he replied. There is a young woman about 35 miles northeast of here in a place called Paddle River. Her family name is Fridel. But there may be one drawback. She is Polish."

John smiled. "But that's perfect. I'm Polish too."

He finished up his fall work and when snow came and brought farming to a standstill, he made plans to begin his wife hunting excursion.

Early one December day in 1921, with a cutter (a small sleight) and his dependable team of horses, he bundled up against the cold and set off to look for "that Polish girl". All he knew was the family name and the general direction of the Fridel farm somewhere 35 miles northeast of Sangudo.

In 1921 in this part of Alberta, the land had been surveyed into townships and sections with road allowances. These roads were laid out to run due north and south, due east and west, often across swampy land and muskeg, much of which was impassable. The early settlers had to make their own trails on higher ground, often traveling across a homesteaders' fields. Father knew his journey would take him across many of the fenced homesteaders' fields.

When our Dad came to a fenced field, he had to throw off his blankets and undo a wire gate. These gates were barbed wire strung across posts that stood upright when taut, had to be pulled free, laid on the ground, the horses led through, then the wires pulled tight again and secured before he could climb back into his sleigh and head on northeast.

We children liked to have our Dad tell us the story of "those pesky gates." I'm sure each time he told the story; the number of gates he encountered increased. At last count, he opened and closed 35 gates. Each time he came to a farmstead, he asked if they could give him directions to the Fridel farm. Finally just at dusk he arrived at the Fridel's log house at Paddle River.

Little did John Liss know that the young woman he was about to meet would be the best thing that ever happened to him in his life.

He was about to win the lottery!

Sargent-Major John Liss – 1916 – World War I

The Courtship

Mary Martha Fridel, my mother, was born in 1903 in Galicia, Polish Austria, the oldest child of a devout Catholic family. In 1906, the Joseph Fridel family along with a group of relations arrived in St. John, New Brunswick, Canada. Mother was only 3 but she remembers the huge size of the ship and how very seasick she was. She was one of the 69 passengers in steerage on the steamship Mt. Temple, in the below decks area where passengers paying the lowest fares lived, cooked and slept during their Atlantic voyage.

The morning after landing the passengers were all examined by a medical examiner and a civil examiner. By 8:35 P.M., everyone had been processed, put aboard trains and sent on their way to their recorded destinations. The Fridel family had arrived in Canada with $14.00 cash and was now headed for Edmonton, Alberta.

Grandfather Fridel went to work in the Edmonton coal mines, but his health broke down and he decided to move to a homestead at Paddle River (now called Barrhead). Mary completed grade VIII and later worked as a domestic in Edmonton to earn enough money to attend one year of Technical School. The Fridel family of 4 boys and 2 girls lived in a comfortable log house. In the early days a few chickens and a garden provided a meager living. During the winters, Grandfather Fridel worked part time in the coal mines and gradually was able to buy a plough, some harrows, a cow and a few more chickens. Slowly, year by year, the homestead began to provide a spartan living for the family.

In the fall of 1921, Mary and a friend were asked to canvas the community to collect funds for a Christmas tree program. The two girls rode horseback from homestead to homestead and it was almost dark when Mary returned home. Her brother, Stephen, walked over to stable her tired horse.

"Better go in Sis," he smiled. "There's a boyfriend waiting."

Mother walked in to see a good-looking man talking to her father.

He was introduced to her as John Liss from Sangudo. The stranger was invited to stay and he visited for two days. During that time he talked with Grandmother and Grandfather Fridel about farming problems, Polish history and every conceivable subject except why he had come. Our mother told us he never once spoke directly with her.

"But I knew why he was there and I knew he would be back."

And back he came in mid-December. This time he asked Grandfather for his daughter's hand in marriage.

"Is this agreeable with you, Mary?" Grandfather asked.

"Yes," she replied quietly. "It is agreeable with me."

The wedding was planned for February 24, 1922 and it took place in the Fridel's log house with a Catholic priest, Father McIntyre officiating. Only two families of relatives and one close neighbor attended the ceremony but after the ceremony many other neighbors came and everyone danced to the music of a gramophone lent them by the Rawleigh man. Two of my mother's brothers missed much of the celebration because they had to hitch up the team to Grandfather's little sleigh and take Father McIntyre to his next official duty miles away.

The day after the wedding our mother told us she spent the time sewing things she would need on her mother's sewing machine. She knew that it would be many years before she could afford a machine of her own.

A few days later, on a cold winter day, the young 19 year old bride seated herself next to a husband she scarcely knew, bundled up against the cold and in the horse-drawn cutter started off for her new home near Sangundo. Now there were two of them to open those pesky gates!

They arrived at her new home about dusk. Mother remembers that just before they arrived they bounced over the newly laid logs that made the muskeg road allowance passable in summer. "Corduroy," we called it; logs laid tightly side by side across the spongy soil that gave you a tooth-jarring ride but got you across without getting mired in the muck.

The home where Dad brought Mother was a 12' by 12' cabin made of squared tamarack logs. Dad had not yet completed a building on his own homestead and was still living with his father. There was now a small attic where Grandfather Pozarzyski slept and an 8' x 12' lean-to built where Mother and Dad slept. This limited space was the couple's home for two years but everyone got along well. Mother said Grandfather was soft-spoken and pleasant. Every morning, he went to the root cellar and brought up potatoes and one vegetable so she always knew what she would cook that day. That relieved her of one decision; she said it meant a lot to her. Grandfather would see she always had a supply of firewood for cooking and a pail of well water next to the stove. Grandfather had dug that well by hand, cribbed it and attached a windless to haul up the pails of cold clear water.

Life was much like it had been on her parents' homestead; cows to milk, chickens to feed, wood to split and fires to keep burning, ashes to empty, bread to bake, water to haul by buckets from the well, clothes to scrub, there was no end to work. Worst of all was the loneliness. There were no neighbors along the 4 ½ mile trail to Sangudo, no women to visit with. Dad was busy milling lumber and beginning to build a house on his homestead across the road, ½ mile away. Mother looked forward to the time they could have their own place.

Mother's dowry from Grandmother and Grandfather Fridel had been a cow and a calf. In the spring when the days were longer and warmer, it was decided that Mother would take the wagon with a dependable team of horses, drive to her parents' place and bring the cow and calf back to her homestead. Mother looked forward to visiting her family and enjoyed the quiet trip to Barrhead.

Driving back to her new home with the cow and the calf tied behind the wagon, slowed the team of horses. They had to pull the animals along the 35 mile trip. It was getting dark when they finally approached the corduroy road near home, the tired horses were moving slowly.

Mother saw a person on horseback coming towards her. He was waving and acting familiar but in the dusk she couldn't see who it was. As she stood up to get a better view, the reins fell from her tired hands, the weary horses slipped off the corduroy and the wagon slid off the logs into the wet muck.

"My God woman! How can you be a farmer's wife if you can't control a team of horses?"

The person shouting at her was her husband. Mother had never before heard a man yelling at someone. Her own father and brothers were gentle soft-spoken men who never raised their voices in anger. She was startled, shocked, bewildered and stunned. Grandfather Pozarzyski had heard the yelling and came running to see what awful thing had happened.

That was the first time Mother encountered her husband's temper but it certainly would not be the last.

Clearing the Virgin Land

Clearing the timber from the virgin land was a slow, laborious and demanding process. First John selected any trees suitable for lumber. The others he chopped down by various methods; sometimes he barked the trees so they would die and dry up; sometimes he cut the roots so the wind would blow them over. Then the next task was grubbing out the huge roots with an ax and a grub-hoe, finally piling up and burning the debris.

One fall day when he was gathering firewood for the winter, our dad had a terrible accident. He began chopping a dead tamarack tree when the top half of the tree came crashing down on him. He lay unconscious for several hours before Grandfather Pozarzyski found him. What had happened was that woodpeckers had made a nest in the hollow of the tree. It was rotten at that point and the vibrations from the chopping broke the heavy top, smashing down on the unsuspecting woodsman. After that before he began chopping any tree, Father said he always carefully checked the condition of the tree to make sure there were no disastrous surprises.

The tree-cleared virgin sod had to be broken with a heavy breaking plough. Dad's horses were not strong enough for the task but he was fortunately able to hire a team of oxen from a neighbor. The two strong oxen, Bingo and Jingo, trudged back and forth, slowly turning the sod. Father walked behind the oxen, firmly gripping the heavy breaking plough with both hands, the reins draped over his shoulders, as he guided the blade cutting through the tough soil. It was hard, back-breaking work but each trip of the oxen added 12" of arable soil to Father's field. Once the oxen had broken the virgin soil, his own horses could pull the disking plow and harrows across the newly turned ground.

That first summer of working on his homestead Dad cleared four acres, quite an accomplishment for a novice farmer.

Preparing Dad's 160 acre Soldier's Grant for planting was a different problem. The grant was on the Paddle Valley Flats and that necessitated digging deep ditches by hand to drain the wet areas. I remember standing in one of his ditches, so deep that it hid my father and me from view.

It was hard to realize that this land which had been so soggy and wet could catch fire, but it did. For years a ground fire slowly burned in the peaty soil, the distinctive acrid smell permeated the air for a mile. Father was relieved when it finally burnt itself out and he could break the ground and prepare his Soldier's Grant for planting.

It was 1928 before Father was financially able to hire a man with a tractor to break newly cleared land. Many years later when he hired a bulldozer to do the job, Mother said, "That machine did in half a day what it took your father weeks."

Nature's Obstacles

When I realize all the problems that nature threw at the struggling settlers, I marvel at our parents' dedication and tenacity.

In 1919-1920, the winter snows came very early. There was not enough feed for the cattle. Dad salvaged the hay that had been piled on the roofs of some buildings and chopped young willows and birches for the animals' survival fodder.

One summer root rot appeared on the flats. The grain came up, then wilt destroyed the crop. Another year a promising crop was destroyed by a mite. Then a noxious weed called hemp took over the fields.

Early on a plague of snowshoe rabbits ate newly planted fruit and shrubbery, and devoured the newly stacked sheaves of grain. One year there was an early frost and all the grain froze. Another year hail late in the summer damaged 70% of the crop.

Then there was the year of the great Paddle Valley floods. Dad planted his crop on the flats, was flooded out, planted grain a second time, was flooded out again, and replanted a third time.

Whenever my brothers, my sister and I reminisce about those early days on the farm, we admire how much our parents struggled to provide for us. It was not an easy life.

The Births of Stanley, Vlad and Helen

Our mother possessed a special kind of bravery. She knew that when her babies would be born she would probably face the ordeal at home with no one but her husband or a woman neighbor to help. The nearest hospitals were in the bigger towns long and difficult miles away. Doctors were a rarity in the remote areas of Alberta but in our community the homesteaders felt especially fortunate because a young doctor had recently moved into the Sangudo area, a Dr. Harris.

It was 36 degrees below zero in a raging blizzard on February 16, 1923 when Mother announced quietly to our Dad,

"John, I think you had better send Grandfather for the doctor. I think the baby will be here soon."

While Grandfather dressed himself warmly for the journey, Father saddled the little pony he had purchased especially for this very errand. He watched the saddle horse and its rider disappear into the swirling white landscape and said a silent prayer. As the hours dragged by he busied himself carrying wood and water, pacing the cabin and checking on his uncomplaining wife. At last, to the young couple's great relief, Grandfather returned with the young doctor.

Grandfather took over the task of keeping the fires going and our Dad assisted the doctor. Except for the nervousness of the young parents, there were no complications in the delivery of Mother's first son. Everyone was pleased with Stanley Francis, a healthy baby boy.

When the ordeal was over, Father fixed a cup of tea for the tired young doctor.

"I'm glad that is over, Mr. Liss. This is the first baby I have ever delivered," Dr. Harris confessed.

"I'm sure glad you didn't tell me that before we started. I would have been even more nervous. But I'm glad it's over too."

**Stanley Liss in front of home where he was born. Grandfather's
12' x 12' cabin with additions.**

From the bed came Mother's voice. "You two are glad it's over? I'm
the one who's very glad it's over. Isn't our Stanley a lovely baby?"

Stanley had been born in February and Mother was anxious to
have her parents see their new grandson so it was decided they would
go to Barrhead for Christmas, leaving Grandfather behind to do the
chores. The sleigh ride there was enjoyable and uneventful. On the
morning, Dad, Mother and baby Stanley left the Fridel family to return
to Sangudo, the weather was pleasant, but a short time later a strong
wind began to blow and before long a fierce blizzard developed. The
team was having trouble getting through the drifts, the trail was difficult to follow and it was beginning to get very dark.

There was no choice but to find a place to stay overnight and hope
the storm would abate. They stopped at a farm in Mosside and asked
if they could spend the night.

"Yes, but we have no place to stable your horses and no feed for
them."

Dad worried about leaving his team in the open with no fodder
but there was nothing he could do about it.

Mother, Dad and baby were given a bed in a log addition, but the
chinking had fallen out from between the logs and the wind whistled
into the room. It was cold! Mother had run out of diapers for the baby.

It was impossible to sleep until Dad saw a cowhide on the floor and flung it over the bed to give them a measure of warmth.

The next morning the blizzard still raged, nothing to do but press on. Dad took off several of his outer clothes and wrapped them around the baby.

"Mary, you take the reins, keep the baby well-covered and I will walk behind to keep warm."

Every so often he would call out to Mother to ask how she felt.

One time she answered, "Oh! I'm so sleepy. I think I'll sleep for a while."

"My God, Mary! You are beginning to freeze to death. Get out immediately and start walking!"

Mother remembers the hours of plodding through the snow, the cold, the concern for her baby and finally the welcome sight of their little home. Grandfather had been very worried about them and hastily took over care of the tired horses while the weary, hungry family recovered in the warm cabin.

When Mother told us this story she said, "That's the last and only time we ever went to Barrhead for Christmas."

The land Grandfather had homesteaded on in 1916 was 160 acres, ¼ SW 19-57-6. Our Dad has filed on another 160 across the road allowance ½ mile away, SE 24-57-7. During the 2 years Mother, Dad and Stanley were living with Grandfather in his tiny log house, Dad had been busy on his quarter section building a sturdy two-story house. In 1924, he moved his wife and son into their new home.

That summer my brother Arthur Vlad was born. When Mother knew she was expecting she went to great efforts to see the doctor regularly. Early in August, she went for a final check-up.

"Two weeks to go, Mrs. Liss. This time we will be ready and I'll be there early."

Because the doctor would be coming to the house Mother decided that she should thoroughly clean the house while she felt well. She pumped and heated water, washed the floors and walls, moved the furniture, scrubbed and scoured and by evening tired but pleased with her efforts, she fell into a satisfying sleep.

In the early dawn, she awoke suddenly with acute pain.

"This must be a false alarm," she thought. "The doctor had said two weeks ago go," but the pains did not diminish, instead they increased with alarming rapidity. She knew she would soon be delivering. Grandfather was again sent on his pony to alert a neighbor and bring the doctor.

Our dad said he never forgot that August morning. The air was oppressive and stifling, not a flicker of a breeze in the unnatural stillness, no sound except for a large blue fly buzzing outside the window screen.

He watched feeling very helpless as his wife's pains came closer and closer. He looked at her perspiring face, clenching and unclenching his tight fists.

"Is there anything I can do for you, Mary?" he asked.

"Oh yes, please! I would like a drink of water."

Father grabbed the dipper and ran to the water pail. The water pail was empty. He seized the empty pail and ran to the well house, grasped the pump handle and began to move it furiously up and down.

Nothing happened. The pump had lost its prime. The pump leather had dried and shrunk and there was no water in the cylinder to start the suction process. He ran around looking for some fresh water to prime his pump, finally ten minutes later he dashed into the house sloshing water all the way.

He stopped in amazement. Mother had given birth. At the actual moment of birth, Mother had been completely alone. Father tied the baby's cord and proceeded to put things in order. The first person to come by was a neighbor from 3 miles away. "I came as fast as I could, but I see I wasn't fast enough," she said.

By the time the doctor arrived in the early afternoon, Mother and baby were resting peacefully.

The doctor checked his patient and baby boy and complimented our dad. "Everything seems in order Mr. Liss. You put your previous experience to good use."

I, my mother's third child was also born at home in the winter of 1927. This time Father, several neighbors and a new doctor, Dr. Chisholm were all present, which was a blessing because I was a difficult birth. One of the neighbors who came to help was Mrs. Lund, a very capable woman who assisted her husband in delivering calves. Mother said when the baby was passed to her, she looked most uncomfortable. The doctor noticed and said, 'Better take the baby Mr. Liss and give Mrs. Lund another job." Calves she knew. Babies she didn't. But I was told that I was not a pretty baby and that when Grandma Fridel saw me, she said, "You poor child. At least your mother will love you."

The doctor who delivered me was Dr. Chisholm, the only doctor between Stony Plain and Whitecourt, a distance of almost 100 miles.

He was kindly remembered by his many patients as he tended this wide spread district.

During the five years from their marriage in 1922 to 1927, the countryside was improving. New settlers were moving in. The trails through the bush were straightened out. Homesteaders could work off their taxes by doing roadwork. With axe and shovel, they chopped trees, drained low spots, dug ditches, then reported their work hours to the local counselor for tax credit. Each little improvement was welcomed by the farmers. "It's better than it used to be," they would say when a muck hole had been drained and filled in.

And there were plenty of those muck holes. At every low spot in the trail, at the bottom of each hill, a big mud hole would develop after each rain. There was no way to detour around these mud holes because of the steep ditches on either side of the trail. The high wagon wheels sank into the mud and made deep ruts in the wet soil, then as it dried, the soil hardened into concrete-like clay masses. In the next rain the wheels deepened the ruts even more. Our dad would take his shovel and go out after each rain to level and fill in the ruts nearest our farm. I think he actually enjoyed the job. He could see immediate results and he knew he would get credits on his municipal tax bill.

When Mother was asked what were the worst things about early homesteading days, she replied, "The loneliness and the poor roads."

The Fire

Stanley, Vlad and Helen. In the background is the house that burnt.

Mother and I sat in the living room talking about our early farm days. I asked, "Of all the things that have happened on the farm, what memory is the strongest for you?" Tears came to her eyes.

"It's when I thought my children had burnt in the fire." After 60 years that horrible memory still overcame her.

This is the story our parents told us of that awful day when they thought they had lost their three children in a house fire.

It was 1928. Things were picking up and the future looked promising. By now there was a solidly built frame house on Dad's homestead. Every evening Grandfather Pozarzyski walked the ½ mile from his cabin to help with the chores. He and Mother by hand milked the 12 cows. Now they had cream to sell. Grandfather trapped weasels and muskrats and that helped financially. Dad worked long hours, daylight to dark, clearing and cultivating his land and it was producing fair crops. The herd of cattle was increasing. Things were getting better.

Then calamity struck! Early one morning on market day, Dad decided to ship several head of stock to the stockyards at the railroad, a distance of 4½ miles. There was still no road to Sangudo, only a narrow track through the brush.

The cattle refused to leave the farm so it was decided that Mother would drive the buggy with an old cow tied behind, hoping the herd would follow. Dad was on horseback driving the animals and Grandfather was on his pony to take care of the stragglers. But they could not keep the cattle together, so Grandfather was sent back to the farm to enlist the aid of two hired men who had been helping with haying. When the two men arrived they said they had left the three children sleeping upstairs. Stanley was 5 years old, Vlad was 3 and I, Helen, was 1 year old. When Mother reached the top of a hill, about 2 miles from home, she looked back towards the north and saw smoke rising on the flats in the direction of our farm.

She shouted to Dad about it.

"Don't worry," he called back. "We had some brush fires burning the day before in that direction and the wind must have rekindled the fire."

When Mother looked again, the smoke was worse and she became uneasy so Dad asked Grandfather to investigate and he galloped back to the farm. Mother had a bad feeling and she also turned around and started back to the home. Dad and the two hired men continued on driving the reluctant cattle.

It was shipping day at Sangudo so many farmers were taking cattle to the railroad stock yards. The first person Mother met was Mr. Eickhorn Sr. who was having trouble with a cow that wouldn't lead.

"Did you come across the flats," Mother asked.

"No" he replied.

The next person she met, she asked him the same question and if he had seen a fire.

"Yes," he replied, "They tell me it's a family named Liss." Mother didn't know who the man was but the third person she met was a close neighbor, Herman Rhese. When Mother asked if our house was gone, he said,

"I am sorry to tell you Mrs. Liss, it is all gone."

"What about the children?"

Tears streamed down Herman's face. "I'm sorry to tell you they are all gone." Mother remembered him saying "Don't drive too fast Mrs. Liss. There is nothing you can do."

After that her mind went blank until she arrived at the burning house and saw the neighbors standing around. Mrs. Westburg, Sr. was crying. Mother thought "Why is she crying? That won't bring my children back."

The neighbors said when they arrived, Grandfather was rolling on the ground in hysterics, sobbing next to a table and four chairs he had somehow dragged from the fire.

"Dead! All dead! The children are all dead and I couldn't save them."

Mother's brother, Uncle Frank Fridel came up, put his arms around her and said, "I'm sorry Sis."

Mother stood dazed. Then they heard voices coming from the hay field. Uncle Frank said, 'Look Sis. There are your children." There coming across the yard was Vlad and behind him Stanley, struggling to carry his 1 year old sister. The children were alive!

Mother said that now that the children were safe nothing else seemed to matter.

Dad meanwhile had finally gotten the cattle to the stockyards, then went to the store and Post Office. A neighbor came up to him in the post office and said, 'John, you better go home right away."

Dad said, "What's wrong? What's the matter?"

"I am so sorry to tell you your house has burnt down."

"And the children? Are the children safe?"

Tears came to his eyes. "John, I am so very sorry. Your children are all gone too. John, I'm so sorry."

Dad said he immediately started for home. He was numb! He met another neighbor in a Model T Ford, the first car in the countryside. The driver called out "John! Thank God your children are safe. They were in the hay field." Dad could not describe his great relief except to say, "Thank God. Thank God!". This is what our parents told us about the fire.

When Grandfather galloped back to the house, he found a blazing fire in the upper story where the children slept. He thought he heard them crying. He tired frantically to get up the stairs but the smoke was too dense. He wrapped a wet towel around his face but he still couldn't get through the smoke. In desperation he tried to save some of the family's newly purchased furniture and managed to throw out an oak table and 4 dining chairs. In a very short time the whole house was ablaze.

Our parents never knew what started the fire. They knew that before everyone left with the cattle, the kitchen stove had been out. There was no other source of heat. Matches were always kept hidden from the children.

They speculated that a man with a tractor who had been breaking land for them, had slept upstairs and may have been careless with his matches. Vlad being a curious lad, may have found a match and lit it. Dad had been doing carpentry work in one of the upstairs rooms and there was a big pile of shavings on the floor, and according to Stanley that is where the fire started.

When Stanley wakened and saw the fire, he carried up a pail of water from downstairs and tried to put the fire out. Grandfather later said he had seen spilled water on the treads during his futile attempts to go up the stairs. When Stanley saw the fire was quickly spreading, he wakened his one year old sister, Helen, and got his brother and sister out of the burning house. There was no one around so he took them to the hay field where he thought everyone was working. When he saw no one was there he led his brother and carried his baby sister back to the house.

What to do now? Give up? Quit and move away? Never! Father intended to homestead this land and nothing was going to stop him. He never once considered that he would do anything but rebuild his house.

That night we slept with neighbors. The next day our dad carefully looked over the few buildings on the farmstead. He decided that the well house was best suited to become our temporary home. Grandfather cleaned and swept out the tiny building and we moved in.

It was a rough framed simple structure about 15 ft. by 15ft. that had been built over the well to protect it from the elements. There was no insulation, no foundation, and a rough floor of planks, but it had a roof that didn't leak and would keep the family out of the rain.

Our other neighbors soon heard of our misfortune. They brought us whatever they could spare from their meager belongings. Before long we had a stove, some dishes, a few blankets and bits of clothing. These together with the table and chairs Grandfather had saved gave us a place to cook, a place to eat and a place to sleep. Our parents were grateful for every little gift.

The day after the fire, Mother said she cried for the first time. She was washing a few dishes and she looked for a dish rag. She had none. She thought, "Maybe there will be a rag left on the clothesline." The day before the fire, she had done her weekly wash and had asked Stanley to bring in the clothes. Stanley was so conscientious and thorough that he had brought in every last scrap of cloth.

Mother said she sat down and cried. "I have nothing. I don't even have a dish rag."

Mother put great responsibility on her oldest child. "Stanley was born mature," she would often say.

"But this time I wish he had missed one small scrap of rag."

Mother said that Stanley, her oldest child had been denied the luxury of a childhood. He was the first born and responsibilities far beyond his years were forced upon him. At two years, he was baby sitting his brother, Vlad. At four he was helping regularly with the household chores. By the time he was five he was left in charge of my brother and me while Mother went to help in the fields.

After the fire, Mother found she was away from the little home more and more. As soon as she left our tiny shack, I would begin to cry and poor Stanley was always looking for ways to keep me quiet. One day he found the solution on Mother's little dresser. Father had only recently managed to save enough money to buy Mother a small belated diamond engagement ring. Stan discovered that if he put the ring on my finger, the sparkle of the diamond intrigued me and I would stop crying. But the ring was too big for my tiny finger and kept falling off and I would start to cry again. Obviously, the ring must be made small enough to stay on my finger, so Stanley got a hammer and pounded the ring to bend it into shape. When Mother came home from work I wasn't crying, but the diamond wasn't in her ring either. The little stone had fallen out of its setting when my brother was reshaping it. Mother, Father and Grandfather swept all the cracks in the well-house floor. They sifted and resifted the dust and searched the place thoroughly but they never found the tiny diamond.

Dad said that after the fire, Grandfather was never the same. He loved his 3 grandchildren and the trauma and stress of the fire broke his spirit. He died two years later, after a riding accident.

Grandfather had ridden his pony to Sangudo for groceries and the mail. He was on the narrow trail through the brush when a car came towards him. Cars were very rare in those days and horses were not used to them. Grandfather's pony was a quiet one but at the sight of the strange car, the terrified animal shied, backed up against some fallen trees, and horse and rider fell, pinning Grandfather's leg between the saddle and a log. The man with the car extricated Grandfather and brought him home. Dad could see it was a compound fracture. He put splints on the leg and got Grandfather to Edmonton, the nearest hospital. Grandfather seemed to be recovering well and after a few weeks was ready to be sent home to the farm. Then unexpectedly he died of a blood clot. He was only 69.

The funeral was held in Edmonton. Dad said he wanted his two sons to attend their Grandfather's funeral. Stan would have been 6, Vlad 5.

"I have no pants the boys could wear," Mother said.

Dad thought for a moment. "Go to Mrs. Merryweathers, the secretary of the municipality. She has 2 sons about Stanley and Vlad's ages. Maybe she can lend you some pants for the boys."

When Mother explained her problem to Mrs. Merryweather, the lady went into a back room and returned holding up two pairs of pants.

"Will these do?" she asked. "Oh! No! One of these has a patch. Let me see if I can find a better pair."

She again went into the back room and soon returned with two pairs of pants.

"I think these will look respectable on your sons Mrs. Liss."

Dad said when they got to Edmonton, Stanley and Vlad sat on the edge of the sidewalk and watched in amazement as car after car went by on the smooth street. They were spellbound watching these strange machines, something they had never seen in Sangudo. Dad said their heads turned left and right, back and forth in wonder.

Mother said she missed Grandfather. He had been kind, gentle and sympathetic and a great help in easing her burden with the never-ending farm work. She said he loved playing with his three grandchildren. He would come home from the store and tell us he had candy in one of his pockets, then watch with delight as we searched for the pocket with the prize.

Grandfather Pozarzyski willed his ¼ section of land not to his wife or any of his children, but to our Mother, a final gesture of the love and respect between father-in-law and daughter-in-law.

Grandfather, John Pozarzyski, 1858-1929 is buried in St. Joaquin Cemetery in Edmonton, Alberta.

After the fire, the immediate task of re-building the house took precedence. Fortunately there was a small amount of insurance, a $250 policy and in addition the Soldier Settlement Board had taken out a policy for $800. Once again our Dad cut and milled lumber. Once again he began building a home for his family. He did all his own carpentry with only a few basic tools and a determined will.

I remember our Dad taking the bent nails from the fire and carefully pounding them straight with a hammer against a flat iron. "Waste not, want not" was a family motto. We certainly did not waste, but in material things we did want.

When Grandfather Pozarzyski willed his quarter section to Mother, our parents wanted to keep the land. Dad had recently acquired a second homestead adjacent to his soldier's grant and original homestead. With Grandfather's land, they now owned 640 acres of Paddle Valley acreage. But the family was hard pressed for cash and needed money badly. Reluctantly, they decided to sell Grandfather's 160 acres. In 1931, they sold the fertile quarter section to an immigrant family from the Ukraine, Michael Kuchevich and John Oksukevich for $2,000 dollars with $700 dollars down and the balance to be worked off in labor.

All of us regarded this family as part of our own family. Whenever something special happened to us kids, we would walk the ½ mile across the road to share our good news with Pani Kuchevich. She would fold her hands in prayer, look upward and say, "Oh! Tank you Got. Tank you Got!" She was frugal, yet she always had a round peppermint candy for us. She was a dear! She was a tiny person, thin and bent with osteoporosis and hard work, yet she lived into her 90's, always alert, always smiling, always pleased to see any of the Liss family.

Saugus, March 21-1931

On or before June 1st 1931 we jointly and severally promise to pay to John Ross of Saugus Saseuw at his home in the vicinity of Saugus the sum of Fifty-five ($55⁰⁰) Cash with interest at 8% after maturity

In the alternative we jointly and severally undertake to pay John Ross the said sum by furnishing him with the labour of our son John Oksiukiewicz from the date to June 1st next, the wages for the period to be the total sum of fifty-five dollars ($55⁰⁰)

Her
Juljanja Kucewicz
Mark

Mark
Micheeel
Kucehuwich

Stephen Stanley Heintz

witness

Grandfather Pozarsyski's homestead "Agreement for Sale"
to Michael Kuchevich – 1931.

The Depression

Our parents decided that in the future, their children would be born in a hospital, no more of this "at home" stuff. In October, 1929 mother was in the Royal Alexandra Hospital in Edmonton awaiting the birth of her fourth child, Edward Vitold, when her room-mate, reading the Edmonton Journal announced,

"I see the New York stock market crashed. I wonder what that will mean to my husband's job."

Mother said with certainty, "Well that won't affect me. I'm a farmer's wife."

Years later she said, "Was I ever wrong. Little did I know then how our life would change, how wide-reaching the depression would be on my family."

Dad bought Mother a nice radio, long and short wave, as a gift for Edward's birth. It would be many years before he could afford another expensive present.

After the crash, prices fell for farm produce. When Mother delivered her weekly 5 gallon cream can to the railroad station in Sangudo, it brought an average price of $1.00. If the cream soured, the price was .85¢. Eggs brought 5¢ a dozen. One year it cost our parents 6¢ a bushel to thresh their barley, but the market price they received was 4¢ a bushel.

When our dad took a double box load of grain to the elevator, he brought home one 98 lb. sack of flour, 10 lb. of sugar and 35 cents change – nothing more than this for a summer's harvest!

All across the country, men were out of work. They would walk from farm to farm asking for any kind of a job. Our parents couldn't pay them for work but they would give them food and often let them sleep overnight. In the winter the men laid their bedrolls under the kitchen table, in the summer they could sleep in the hay barn if they promised not to smoke. On one occasion our parents let one of those poor unfortunates bring his bedroll upstairs, the area where all of us youngsters had our bedrooms. A few days after he left, we unhappily awoke to find bites all over our bodies. "Bedbugs," Mother said. The only way we had to eradicate those elusive, disagreeable, pesky creatures was to spray our mattresses and liberally soak the tufts and edges with coal oil. The upstairs reeked of the strong smell of kerosene but eventually we did dispose of our unwanted "guests" and once again we were able to sleep in peace.

One man, Wesley Barnard, had worked for our dad one summer. He came back in the winter.

"Just give me enough money for tobacco and I'll work for you," he begged.

He and his brother had been asked by their parents to leave home because the parents had no money to feed their sons.

Men rode the rails looking for work. Mother told me about the time she saw a freight train pull into Rochfort Bridge station. The men on top of the boxcars threw off their bedrolls as the R.C.M.P. walked along yelling "Off! Off!" Then the men picked up their bedrolls, walked to the farthest section of the train and climbed back on. The R.C.M.P. walked past purposely ignoring the men they had just ordered off.

Our dad had purchased a small lot in the village of Sangudo in mother's name. It was always referred to as "Mother's Lot." The plan was that when the time came for us children to go to High School, 4 ½ miles away, Dad would build a cabin for us to stay there overnight during inclement weather. Four and a half miles can seem like a mighty long and difficult walk if you are trudging through snow in a blowing snowstorm.

Mother's lot was SW 19-57-6-5 but Dad never got to build us our shelter. The lot went to tax sale because the taxes were in arrears. The total mount of the unpaid taxes was $50.69. When you have little cash and you have to decide whether to pay taxes or buy food for your family, there is no choice. For many years, I resented that someone else owned "Mother's Lot."

About once a month, Dad would hitch up his team to the wagon and leave early in the morning to take care of business in Sangudo. We kids eagerly awaited his return in the late afternoon, hoping he would have a treat for us, which he usually did. He would bring out a 5¢ Rose Marie chocolate bar that Mother cut into nine even pieces. On rare occasions, Dad had two candy bars for us, a Rose Marie and an Oh Henry for all of us to share.

"Other men go to the beer parlour but I treat my children first.

Maybe some day Mother and I will be able to enjoy a cold beer on a hot day." I remember him often saying.

My sister, Valeria and I both remember a treat from Mrs. Harris. She was a lady who lived alone a mile north of us, a recluse who seldom spoke to people. Mrs. Harris had thick, straight, grayish brown hair that hung stiffly half-way down her shoulders. A brown beat-up looking slouch hat partly covered her face. Her head was always tilted downward, her eyes never looked directly at you and when she spoke her voice was hesitant and uncertain, a leather gloved hand shaded her face from view whenever she approached someone.

About once a month we would see her trudging back from town, a gunny sack full of groceries on her back. Valeria and I were picking high bush Pembina cranberries on the river hill when Mrs. Harris came by. We spoke to her and she stopped, put down her pack and visited with us, never once shading her face with her gloved hand. After a few minutes, she reached into her pack and handed us a small can of sliced pineapple.

Valeria and I were so proud when we showed Mother our prize. She cut the slices into nine pieces and thanks to Mrs. Harris we all had our first ever taste of pineapple.

In the years from 1929 until the war broke out in 1939 we never had much cash, but neither did any of our neighbors so it seemed like a normal situation. I vividly recall our dad searching for three cents to be able to mail a letter. All of us saved, reused, traded, borrowed, mended or did without.

When the T. Eaton catalogue arrived in the fall, we dreamed. Everyone referred to it as the "wish book," – all those pretty clothes, fancy shoes and lovely coats – would we ever be able to afford those?

As our outer coats became threadbare and worn looking, Mother ripped the seams apart, saved the threads, ironed the seams flat, reversed the material and resewed it to create a new-looking garment for another season's wear.

Vlad was in Grade X when he came home from Sangudo High School one September and announced,

"We have a new teacher who will teach us music. He will teach me to play the slide trombone if I can buy one."

"How much will it cost," our dad asked.

"Seventeen dollars."

"We have been saving money for Mother to buy a new winter coat. Her old one is worn and thread-bare and not very warm. She really needs a new coat."

Mother spoke up, "This is the first time we have had a teacher who has offered to teach our children music. Let's use the money we've saved to buy Vlad a trombone. I can wear my coat for one more winter."

She turned her old brown coat inside out, Vlad got his slide trombone, practiced regularly without being told and pleased us all with melodies we could recognize.

Mother never complained about her reversed old brown coat but I would always notice that the belt she had not been able to alter looked shabby.

One Saturday Mother said, 'You can have the egg money this week."

I carefully packed eighteen eggs in a bucket of oats, careful to position them in the spongy seeds so they wouldn't break when I took them to the store in the village. Each egg would bring me 1¢. When I carried my bucket into the store, I set it on the counter. The clerk, her name was Anne, idly ran her fingers through the oats.

"Oh!" she exclaimed. "I just broke one of your eggs."

My heart sank. There went 1¢ and there was nothing I could do about it. It wasn't fair!

My brother Edward liked to visit with a bachelor, Nathan Duff, who lived west of Dad's homestead. One summer day Ed came into the kitchen, visibly shaken, his face white.

"What is it? What happened?" our worried Mother asked.

"I saw a bear," Ed replied.

Bears were a rarity in our area but no one doubted that Ed had indeed seen a bear. Our Dad gave us a logical explanation of why a bear was in the woods of his undeveloped land.

About 40 miles west of us near Whitecourt and across the Athabasca River a giant forest fire had raged all summer long. It appeared to be spreading, smoke and the smell of burning forest blanketed our countryside. Dad said the animals sensed the impending danger and were fleeing to safer ground.

The rumor we heard about that fire was that it had been deliberately set by men out of work, hoping they could then apply to the government to fight the fire and receive some sorely needed compensation. We never knew if the rumor was true but desperate men do desperate things during a depression.

1930 – John Liss payment receipt for arrears in taxes.

Groceries were charged all through the year, until the Fall, when harvesting brought in some income in order to pay off the debt.

Root Picking

The Chippewa Indians still used part of Dad's land for their ceremonies and sweat baths, so Dad hired them to pick roots and rocks on his newly broken land but he soon found they weren't very dependable. I remember Big John and Little Sam. Funny names, I thought because Big John was little and Little Sam was big. One noon Dad invited the two men to join us at the kitchen table for a meal. They sat down silently, ate silently, then stood up abruptly and said,

"Me Go!"

They smelled strongly of wood smoke and when they left the heavy odor remained downstairs for hours. Our dad always treated the Indian peoples with respect and they in turn respected him. They never called him Mr. Liss, it was always "John".

During the summer school holidays, we children were given the task of piling the loose roots and rocks onto a "stoneboat" a flat table-sized sled on skids that was pulled across the field by two horses. Father paid us for this chore, a penny apiece for each stoneboat load, and we worked willingly for the incentive. Cash, even a penny was a lot of money to a kid in those depression times. Invariably, we spent our fortune at the candy counter in the corner of the village barber shop. The barber always waited patiently behind the glass while we spent mouth-watering minutes deciding from among the penny items. Should it be a red or a black licorice whip? Or a box of licorice pipes? Some jawbreakers or bubblegum? Or a package of maple buds or some multi-colored jelly beans?

But sometimes after a long, hot day of root and rock picking, it seemed as if the task was endless. Where did all these roots and rocks come from?

"Why," I said to Father in disgust, "When you choose your homestead, did you have to pick land with so many trees and rocks on it?"

"Well, my dear," he replied. "The trees are here because we have good soil and the rocks came with the glacier 10,000 years ago."

Nothing excited us more than finding Indian relics among the rocks and roots. We would run eagerly to show Father our prize. Usually we found crude arrowheads, sometimes axes and scrapers. Beneath many of the larger poplar trees there would be a hard grey and black ball that we knew must be Indian pemmican. Hadn't we learned in school that the Indians stored a cache of pemmican underneath big trees for future use? We boiled the mass for half a day without seeing any change in its appearance. Later, a visiting professor from the University of Alberta told us our "pemmican" was nothing more than a common poplar tree fungus. What a disappointment!

The United Farmers
of Alberta

In 1935 in the midst of the depression, a political party, the Social Credit, led by William Aberhardt promised $25.00 a month to every person in Alberta if he were elected.

"How can he do that?" Grandmother Fridel said. "But maybe he can, so I'll vote for him." So did many others and the party swept into power.

Fifty four years later mother recalled a conversation she and I had after Aberhardt made his promise.

"What do you have to do to get the $25.00?" I asked her.

"Nothing," she replied. "Just vote for him."

"How can you get something for nothing?" I said.

"At eight years old you could see the fallacy but most people could not see through his improbable promise."

John Liss said if you put a "Social Credit" sign on a jackass, people would vote for it. The Social Credit Party remained in power in Alberta for over thirty years, but we never saw our $25.00.

It was during this period that our father became interested in politics and the cooperatives that became the salvation of the working class farmers.

Farmers in Canada at the beginning of the 20th century were completely at the mercy of the big grain companies, the packing concerns and the dairy cartels. The farmers were determined to form an organization to lessen their dependence on big business. They formed a strong organization called the United Farmers of Alberta (the U.F.A.) and they began setting up many cooperatives.

Our father realized the absolute necessity of a strong farm organization to look after the farmers' interests and he plunged whole-heartedly into the work. He took long trips with his team, visiting distant farmers outlining the benefits of cooperatives and setting up meetings. Strong opposition came from some businesses. He was called a troublemaker, a Bolshevik, a Communist, was threatened to be tarred and feathered, and sometimes denied rental of a hall. Even the Deputy Minister of Agriculture tried to dissuade him from organizing a seed cooperative. The local banker gave him a severe tongue-lashing for interfering with local merchants' profits. Dad referred to the banker as "that contemptible skunk."

During Dad's travels, Mother remained on the farm to take care of us kids and the farm chores because she believed in the work her husband was doing. As a direct result of banding together and eliminating all the middlemen, the farm co-ops were able to grow and sell produce at far lower prices than the big companies. It was a welcome sight, when one fall day, a box car full of fruit from British Columbia pulled into the railroad siding in our little village. The co-ops brought in apples, onions, salt and flour at reasonable prices that the farmers could afford. For the first time ever the Liss family had apples, big red firm Macintosh apples, one a day, every day until we emptied the big wooden crate. To this day, I remember the pleasant smell of that shiny fruit and the pleasure of biting into a delicious crunchy MacIntosh apple.

Every fall, from then on, the farm co-operatives delivered a box car load of British Columbia fruit to all the small villages on our railroad line. Our father had been subjected to abuse, ridicule and road blocks but he and a few like-minded farmers had persevered and succeeded in bringing fresh produce directly from the growers to the farm customers.

Our lives were better thanks to the farm "co-ops" and the efforts of John Liss and a few strong dedicated individuals.

Alberta Wheat Pool

Office of the
President

JOHN LISS

Because a group of grain producers took the initiative to solve their problems through mutual action in 1923, the Alberta Wheat Pool is observing its fiftieth anniversary this year. Our present members salute those original contract signers whose constancy and loyalty helped build "their association" into a great organization.

On behalf of the membership I pledge Alberta Wheat Pool to continue the pursuit of objectives laid down by you and your fellow founding members. This memento is presented as a token of our esteem for your actions and beliefs.

Yours sincerely,

G. L. Harrold

G. L. Harrold

Letter of appreciation to John Liss for his work in organizing a grain co-operative in 1923.

The Soldier Settlement Board

When we were growing up there was always a shortage of money. Over the years, we would hear our father cursing that "God-dammed Soldier Settlement Board," but not until I was an adult did I realize the full story behind his anger.

When our dad received his soldier's grant after World War I, the government allowed him to borrow $3,000.00 to be paid back with interest. These monies were to assist the veterans in buying necessary equipment and supplies to begin farming. Each expenditure had to be approved and verified by the department. At first Father was optimistic that he could manage his payments but after the 1928 fire and the 1929 depression there was little cash. He paid his school and municipal taxes and bought only the barest of necessities for his children. He made his S.S.B. interest payments but they wanted more. The S.S.B. asked him to sign a paper giving the agency title to his land, assuring father he was in no danger of losing his property. John knew of several veterans whose land had been seized by the S.S.B.

"I'll see you in Hell before I sign such a paper," he declared.

John learned from his neighbors that the S.S.B. regarded him as a troublemaker and that they planned to seize any cattle or crop he took to market and then take over his farm.

In his memoirs he wrote, "I prepared for the worst. I examined my 303 rifle, secured ample ammunition and was prepared to defend my home and family to the death."

He wrote directly to the Prime Minister of Canada, MacKenzie King.

"Last fall my crop was seized by the Soldier Settlement Board and I have since been subjected to inhuman and heart-breaking humiliation. The S.S.B. has accused me of making only interest payments on my loan. They state I have animals to sell and could be paying off the principal. To dispose of any of my animals with a 4¢ cut in market price and deprive my farm of breeding stock would be the height of folly and stupidity.

I have other creditors to satisfy – doctor and hospital bills, school and municipal taxes to pay. Frost ruined my crop in 1935. I am practically destitute. If my wife had not worked in the fields, side by side with me, often forced by circumstances to neglect home and the little ones to do so, we would be even worse off. We have denied ourselves cream and butter to have more to sell for desperately needed cash to buy food for my children.

We lack many necessities. We have mixed wheat chop with flour to make it go farther in bread-baking. We have no furniture but what I have made from our own lumber. We lack bedding and warm clothing. My children wear clothes others refer to as rags. With what little cash I receive, I must care for my children first. That is my God-given obligation.

Even a criminal is given his constitutional right to defend himself before a fair and impartial judge. What chance did we have to defend ourselves before seizure of our crop?

I am not asking for anything else but a square deal for myself and my family. I will fulfill my obligation to you in good time, but leave us in peace."

The Soldier Settlement Board collectors did stop harassing John Liss and eventually he paid off his debt. In later years, thinking back about the S.S.B., Dad said it would have been better for him if he had not had anything to do with that agency. When he took out his loan, he was optimistic and eager but hard times and the harassment he endured were an emotional drain.

"I was sure relieved when I got rid of that pain in the neck," he said. "But then it was an S.S.B. man who told me about Mother, so some good came of it, after all."

Alberta Government Telephones

In our living room we had a radio that had A batteries and B batteries. When the batteries were new, we could listen to the Lux Radio Theatre and the Lone Ranger. When the batteries were low the radio was turned on only for the 12:00 o'clock and 8:00 o'clock news. During the 15 minute period when the news was on, absolute silence was the rule. No one dared to speak!

Vlad had a crystal set. As he sat in a corner of the living room with his ear-phones on, he would occasionally burst out laughing. I envied him and wished the rest of us could share his fun. One summer day I did indeed share in his fun.

A telephone line, the Alberta Government Telephones, had been strung in our community about 1935 but we could not afford to subscribe for several years. One Sunday when everyone was away and Vlad and I were home alone, he said,

"I'm going to tap into that telephone line but I'll need your help. I've got an idea of how we can listen in to anyone talking on the party line phones."

We walked the ¼ mile up the hill from our house to the roadway where the telephone line ran. Vlad climbed a ladder and attached a copper wire to the main line. I didn't understand what he did; my job was to hold the coil of copper wire which we then carefully unrolled down the hill and into the house. Then my brother attached the copper wire to the ear-phones of his crystal set.

"Here you hold one up to your ear and I'll hold the other."

We laughed out loud when we heard our neighbors talking. After a few minutes one lady said,

"There's a lot of static on this line. What do you suppose it is?"

"I bet I know where it is and who is doing it," the other lady said.

"Oh, no you don't," Vlad and I yelled back. Of course they couldn't hear us, but what a gleeful Sunday we had hearing them. We were careful to dismantle our invention and hide all the evidence before our parents came home. A few years later we could afford to subscribe to the Alberta Government Telephone but we never had as much fun as our copper wire caper.

When we became subscribers to the party line, our wooden telephone was fastened to the kitchen wall behind Mother's chair. Our "number" was three longs and a short, three long brisk turnings of the handle, followed by one short ring. The problem was in recognizing your own combination of rings whenever someone called you, so when in doubt, we would pick up the receiver, but so would other subscribers, resulting in a weak delivery and necessitating shouting into the mouthpiece to be heard.

If it rained, our line often went dead. If tree branches blew against the line, static resulted. Not until 1970 when the Alberta Government buried the phone cable did the subscribers have dependable reception and dial telephones. Now we could dial our numbers directly and not have to endure long waits for "Central" to respond to our repeated rings.

Poplar School District #3215

It was 1933 when I started my first day of school at Poplar School, under the care of my two older brothers, Stanley and Vlad. All I remember about that first day was the teacher's name, Miss Wackenhut and that she sat me in a two-seater desk at the back of the room. My seat-mate was Martin Pudar, he sat as far from me as possible and I sat as far from him as possible, crying because I had to sit next to a boy.

Poplar School was 3½ miles away by road, but we could shorten that distance to 3 miles by going across our own land. We walked along the cattle run to Dad's new homestead, through a poplar grove, across two muskegs, then half a mile of muddy trail and a final mile of graded road before we reached the welcome clearing where Poplar School #3215 stood.

Walking across our own land was fun because we had names for spots along the way – the lookout, the gravel pit, Indian sweat bath hill, the weasel traps, tiger lily hill, pheasant meadows and strawberry patch corner. There was a mound by a creek that Valeria and I knew must be an Indian grave. We planned to dig it up someday.

After we left our land, the trail was tedious, a mile of thin black road with dense old poplar tree forest on either side, the monotony occasionally broken by the thrill of seeing a deer dash across the road.

Our little school was constructed like so many in the countryside. We entered into a room where firewood was stored, then opened a second door into the boy's cloakroom. At the opposite side of the room was the girl's cloakroom where the teacher kept her supplies. On the grounds there was a shed for horses, a well with a pump, two toilets, one for boys and another for girls, built a goodly distance apart. Thick forest surrounded the school grounds and we never dreamt of wandering off into that mysterious unknown and we were content to obey the rules and never play off the school grounds.

We had a new teacher for third grade. By now I liked Miss Wackenhut and was sorry to see her leave us.

"Children," our new teacher announced, "I have forms to fill out for the school authorities. Please ask your parents where you were born and let me know tomorrow."

When I asked Mother where I had been born, she replied, "You were born right here." She meant I had been born here in our farmhouse.

Next day, the teacher asked, "And where were you born, Helen?"

I had rehearsed my answer and in a clear, firm voice I replied.

"I was born right here."

Everyone laughed and I could not understand why.

When I was in third grade, Fern Lersburg spanked me. I sat behind her and pulled her hair. She said, "If you do that again I'll spank you."

So I did it again and she spanked me. When I told Mother she said,

"Well, I guess you deserved it."

From grades four to eight, my teacher's name was Miss Sides. She was 19 years old when her father drove her to the farm to be interviewed by our Dad, one of the school trustees. Miss Sides was an excellent teacher who taught us to excel, only our best was good enough. She would accept nothing less and we did our lessons over and over until they were correct and to her satisfaction. I think I rewrote "The Black Hole of Calcutta" and "The Indian Mutiny" three times before May Sides accepted my paper.

If we misspelled a word, we wrote it correctly on the blackboard 10 times. If we misspelled it a second time, we were required to write the word 50 times. "Design" was easy but when I had to write "old-fashioned" 50 times, I figured out how to hold three pieces of chalk between my fingers and hastily scribbled three words at a time when the teacher wasn't looking.

Our school day began at 9:00 A.M. We all stood for the Lord's prayer, then one of us had to read a few verses from the Bible. Some of our students came from homes where the parents were first generation arrivals from Europe and English was not spoken at home. It was painful to listen to these children struggle through their Bible assignment and I felt very sorry for them.

Our school had eight grades in ages from 7 to 16 years. One of the students was the school janitor, and that person, boy or girl, was required to arrive at school by 8:00 A.M. to start a fire in the stove at the back of the schoolroom. Water had to be pumped to fill the drinking pail, firewood needed to be carried into the anti-room, and kindling needed to be chopped.

At noon, the janitors had another job. They were required to pour a ladleful of water onto our hands because Miss Sides insisted our hands were to be washed before we ate our lunch. After school the janitor had to sweep the floors, clean the blackboards, bang the brushes to empty them of chalk and see that the cloakrooms were tidy. The job of janitor was a prestigious one that paid $10.00 a month and was highly sought after in those depression days.

Our Miss Sides was a strict teacher with firm rules of deportment and behavior.

No one ever whispered or turned around in Miss Sides' classroom. One day Vlad shouted, "Airplane!" and I thought "Boy! Is he going to get it." Miss Sides turned, listened, and surprised us all by letting us go outside to watch, as high in the sky, a tiny blot flew over us. After that if any of us ever heard an airplane she would let us go outside and follow the plane until it went out of sight. Years later, we learned these small planes were carrying whitefish from our northern lakes to restaurants in New York City.

One spring day, Miss Sides announced,

"Boys and girls, I have a surprise for you . Next Friday will be a school holiday. There is going to be a movie shown in the Sangudo Hall called 'Snow White and the Seven Dwarfs,' and the school board wants all of you to go and see your first movie. The film is free, so please go."

As I sat watching I could not understand how those figures could walk across the front of the hall. Where did they come from? What was going on?

A high point of our school year was the Christmas Concert. Early in December, we went around to our neighbors selling tickets, 10 cents each or 3 for 25 cents. The teacher used this money to buy an apple and an orange for each child's Christmas stocking. Our parents all came to watch us perform our recitations on a make-shift stage. We older kids whispered, "Who do you think will be Santa Claus this year?" sure we were keeping the secret from the little ones. Valeria at 6 years whispered back, "It's going to be Jenny Anderson again."

The Christmas Concert was always an exciting and happy day. It would be dark when we left for home, an apple and an orange in hand, the anticipation of Christmas Day ahead of us.

When the Christmas holidays were over and school started in

January it seemed as if our days were shorter than ever. Our homestead was about 54 degrees north latitude and those precious daylight hours were all too brief.

During those cold winter days, our father always arose at 6:00 A.M. to light a fire in the kitchen stove. Sometimes I could hear him from upstairs muttering in Polish if the wood was green and wet and would not light. Occasionally I would shudder and hide my head under the covers if I heard that awful swear word "Sac-Ara-Mento." Mother arose about 6:30 to cook her family a breakfast of oatmeal or Sunny Boy Cereal. One winter when we had very little money, Dad chopped up our wheat to make cracked-wheat porridge but it required hours of cooking and Mother always cooked it the evening before to make it palatable. By 7:00 A.M. when the chill was off the air, Dad called upstairs to waken us. Valeria and I dressed rapidly in the dark, chilly air, often pulling on our heavy woolen underwear and outer clothing under the covers, then scrambling down the stairs to the warm kitchen to put on socks and shoes.

A heavy curtain hung at the bottom of the stairs to keep the warm air in the kitchen. But, oh! That upstairs was so cold. The two windows of our room were so thick with hoar frost ½ inch deep that it was impossible to see out. When it wasn't too cold to be in our bedroom, my sister and I were fascinated by the pretty floral pattern the frost made on the window panes.

My two older brothers had their daily chores to perform before coming back in for breakfast; pigs to water and feed, hay to throw to the horses, water to be pumped to fill the big animal watering trough, and firewood to be carried in for the day's supply. My job was to slice the crusty loaves of bread Mother always baked and to make our school lunches. Sometimes we had no filling for our sandwiches but cold sliced potatoes or cooked beets. My oldest brother, Stan, liked thick slices of yellow onion on his sandwiches. "An apple a day keeps the Doctor away, but an onion a day keeps everyone away," he would say. It was sure true! We saved every scrap of waxed paper but if we had none, our sandwiches were wrapped in an old Edmonton Journal. Lunch papers were always carefully refolded and brought home from school.

Eight o'clock was the critical hour when Dad checked the back porch thermometer. That thermometer ruled our lives in the winter. If it registered above 20° below and there was no wind, we would be allowed to leave for school. If it was any colder, or if a blizzard was

51

blowing, he refused to let us leave the farm. If it warmed up before noon, he relented and we could go on to school. We kids really wanted to go to school and my older brothers and I learned that if we blew on that thermometer, we could force that thin red line above that critical minus 20 degree mark. We would hurriedly call our Dad to come and look.

"Now can we go to school? It's warmed up from 20 below."

I think our Dad was well aware of what his three oldest were up to.

During the summers, Dad's work horses had been needed in the fields, but in the winter we could use his most dependable team to pull the cozy little sleigh he had made for our ride to school. He fashioned the back of a Model T into a windproof box on sleigh runners. Two automobile windshields were built at an angle for the reins to come through, giving the driver protection from the wind. Heavy cowhides covered the doors to keep out the cold. Dad had made soft padded seats for us to sit on. Each morning as we were ready to leave, Mother covered us with warm blankets and placed hot rocks wrapped in towels beside our feet. The oldest Liss was the designated driver and the next in age was in charge of the lunch bag. That lunch bag was a big sturdy back pack that Dad had salvaged from World War I.

The oldest child had the authority to discipline the younger siblings if necessary. I looked forward to the day when my two older brothers, Stanley and Vlad would be off to High School and I would be in charge but I never fully realized the responsibilities and duties involved.

As the driver, I had to unhitch the horses and settle them into the school barn while the younger ones rushed into the warm school-house. Sometimes as I unhooked the cold metal traces, I thought my frozen fingers would snap off. Then at the noon hour when everyone sat around the school's warm pot-bellied stove eating their lunches, I had to dress and walk into the cold to feed the two horses their bag of oats. The rule on our farm was, "Feed your animals first. Only then can you feed yourself."

Even though our janitor had started a fire an hour early it was often very cold in our school when we arrived at 9:00 A.M. Miss Sides would march us around and around for fifteen minutes before we settled into our desks. All the big kid's inkwells would be frozen and had to be placed near the stove to thaw. The bucket of drinking water the janitor had filled the night before would be frozen also and needed to be thawed on top of the stove. At the 10:30 A.M. recess we all moved our lunches near the stove, so they too, could thaw.

If it was too cold to play outdoors, we played marbles. The older kids played "knife," flipping the open blades onto the worn wood flooring. Depending on how the knife blades fastened onto the floor, gave you your "points". The person with the highest points was the winner. At noon if it warmed up, we all bundled up and played "fox and goose" in the snow. We tramped out a big circle, divided it into quarters and made one person the fox. He had to try to catch the geese running around the circle, but he could never touch that outer circle. When the snow was wet and heavy we built forts and made snowmen. Miss Sides did not allow us to throw snowballs and we did not dare disobey.

During those long winters, the days were short. It was dark when we left for school and dark when we returned at 4:30. Dad would be waiting for us to unhitch and stable the horses and Mother always had a very welcome bowl of soup or hot milk for us before we took off our school clothes and pulled on our old work clothes to start our evening chores.

My older brothers, Stanley and Vlad, had to chop and crush oats for the pigs, once again throw more hay down from the loft above the barn, fill the horses' feed stalls, and again water had to be pumped to fill that big animal trough.

A fire had to be made in the small stove that was inside the water trough to keep it from freezing over. The chickens in the chicken house had to be fed and watered and the doors carefully locked to keep out the coyotes and foxes and an occasional weasel.

Mother went off to milk the cows and my task was to set the table for supper and put a pot of potatoes on to boil. When Mother carried in the full milk pails we emptied them into the cream separator that was bolted to the kitchen floor. When we finished separating, cream went into the cream can to sell, the skim milk went to feed the pigs. Every evening the cream separator had to be dismantled and the parts washed and well scalded so they would not smell stale and unpleasant.

The job of my younger brothers was to carry in firewood and the kindling which our dad had split, making sure the wood box next to the stove was again full. Whenever I had this job, I stacked the wood at uneven angles so it wouldn't take so many trips from the woodpile to fill the box. Not a very nice example from an older sister!

Finally, chores all done, we children and our parents all sat down at the long table for supper, Father at one end, Mother at the opposite end nearest the stove. All of us seven children sat along the sides in order of our ages. By 8:00 P.M. came my final job, washing the dishes and hoping I had remembered to fill the kettle and heat enough water.

By 8:30 we all gathered in the living room around a small stove while our mother read to us by the light of an Aladdin lamp. Sometimes it was a timely article our dad wanted us to hear, but the best was when Mother in her gentle, soothing voice, would read to us from some novel that had been designated as "good literature." No trash for our Dad's kids! The characters in the stories were very real people to me and as we hurried up to bed at 9:00 o'clock I wondered what would happen to them tomorrow.

Spring was a time of wonder at the rapidity of the changes around us. Our teacher kept a chart showing who saw the first robin, where we saw the first marsh marigold or dandelion, who spotted the first "V" of geese flying north. When some student reported seeing the first green leaf, it seems as if only two days later the whole forest burst out in a mass of shiny green shimmering leaves.

One spring the forests around us were a horrible enormity of voracious insects that ate every living green thing in their relentless march forward. An army of blue-green worms, tent caterpillars by the thousands, appeared from nowhere, advancing like a moving carpet, several feet westward each day, leaving the poplars and willows devoid of greenery. These slimy things fell on our clothing and into our hair and blanketed the road ahead of us. As we walked to school there was no way to avoid them, a slick, slimy, vile residue that was treacherous to traverse. Oh! They were a disagreeable mess! By summer's end we wondered if our forests would ever recover but thankfully next spring, green leaves emerged, so did the tent caterpillars but to a lesser degree. After two years we were grateful these disgusting worms did not reappear.

Spring was the time for the much anticipated music festival at Rochfort Bridge where all the surrounding schools competed. Miss Sides had us practice over and over again and her insistence on doing our best paid off. I won first prize and the accompanying silver cup for best solo and best recitation for the years 1939, 1940, 1941 and 1942. In 1941 I was chosen as best actor (it was fun!) and in 1942 Stanley and I both won cups for best actors. Mother's display shelves didn't get overcrowded because we could keep our cups for only one year but it was a nice feeling to know we had been chosen as winners.

The day of the Rochfort Festival it invariably rained. Hard! Mud splattered across our Model A but our anticipations were high and the rain never dampened our enthusiasm. Our biggest worry was keeping our "good clothes" clean.

One year I was the waiter in "David Copperfield and the Waiter." We needed a pork chop for the play. Mother cut a thick slice of bologna into the shape of a pork chop, breaded it and fried it. After the play was over, we forgot to bring the "pork chop" home. I dreamed of eating that thick piece of bologna but when we retrieved it a week later, it was a mass of green mold. The cup I won for best acting hardly compensated for my lost pork chop.

Our little schools kept us busy with events for us to anticipate. Track meets were also scheduled for the spring. Miss Sides had us practice the running broad jump and the hop-skip and jump every day at noon, encouraging us to try to better our last attempts.

In September, the Sangudo and District Fair Association held its big day in the Community Hall. Again all the local schools exhibited and entries were judged according to category and ages.

Some of the categories for school fair entries were
- an example of hem-stitching.
- a sample of handwriting.
- a handy device made from scrap.
- an invisible garment darn.
- an invisible sock darn.
- a thrift item made from flour sack.
- an article made from old yarn and rags.

We displayed the flowers and vegetables we had grown in the summer. There were categories for baking – bread, cookies, cakes, chocolate fudge and pies. We could hardy wait for the adjudications to finish so we could see if our entries won. I could not understand why the judges were called adjudicators. Why not "judges"?

One year there were only two cake entries. The judge said, "I can't give first prize to either of these. One is undercooked, the other is over-cooked, but I guess I'd rather eat an overdone cake than an underdone cake, so I'll give second prize to the burnt one and third prize to the underdone one."

I remember very clearly the school fair of 1941 because it was such a miserable day, cold, damp and snowing, making our roads a mucky slush. Dad wondered if we would make it back home without getting our Model A stuck. But the good news about that wet September day was that Edward and I each got first prize for our entry of seed wheat; he in the boy's category and I in the girl's. We got a bucket of Dad's fall harvested wheat and carefully selected only the fattest kernels, then we polished each one on a flannel cloth until we filled our pint jars with shiny kernels. When we saw the other sad-looking entries, we knew we would win. And we did!

Our school never had a big enrollment, usually only fifteen pupils, divided in our minds into "big kids" and "little kids." In the summer at recesses and noon our favorite game was "scrub", our version of a ball game. Invariably, Vlad, the biggest kid, would be first up to bat, and his buddy, Joe Hodges, would be catcher. Once, Vlad or Joe were at bat, there was no way we littler kids could get them "out". They would hit the ball hard, run around the bases and be "home" before the rest of us in the field could retrieve the ball. But after Vlad left Poplar school to go to High School in Sangudo, "scrub" didn't seem to be much fun anymore.

Vlad and Joe had a secret spot where they made "hootch". They would disappear into the bushes back of the outhouses, off the school grounds (a no-no) to check on their project. I could never discover what it was or where they hid it. When I asked Vlad what hootch was made of he laughed and said, "Lux toilet soap."

What were they making? Wine?

Every two years, another Liss kid enrolled in Poplar school, first Edward, then Ted and finally Valeria. By the time Johnnie was of school age, Poplar school had closed for lack of pupils. A new school, West Cosmo, opened 2½ miles north east of our home. Today only a small plaque marks the spot where "my" school once stood.

The route to Cosmo School took the children past Uncle Frank's house and his vegetable garden beside the road. Valeria and Johnnie would crawl through the barbed wire fence, help themselves to carrots and sneak off, thinking no one had seen them. Years later when they told Uncle Frank they had been eating his carrots, he smiled.

"Why do you think I planted all those carrots so close to the road?"

Ted liked to tease the girls in school. One day he took Jean Cooper's lunch pail and hung it high in a tree in a way that made it very difficult for her to retrieve it. When the teacher, Mrs. Westerberg heard of Ted's caper, she made him write out 100 times,

"I will not put Jean Cooper's lunch pail up in a tree."

When he went on to Sangudo High School, Ted was very popular with the girls. Now that he was the oldest Liss boy at home, he became the custodian of that beloved Model A, a fact appreciated by the local young ladies.

Ted inherited his father's love of the land. When he finished High School, he went on to Vermilion Agricultural College, for he like his dad, had a dream of becoming a farmer. Because he lived and farmed near our parents and regularly checked on them, John and Mary Liss were able to live with peace of mind to the end of their lives in the home they had built and on the land they had nurtured.

When we were kids picking rocks from Dad's new breaking and piling them onto a stone boat, Edward became intrigued with the Indian artifacts we found in the newly turned soil. He was always an outdoors man. High school algebra didn't interest him – the North West Territories did. When most of us thought of that part of Canada as the Frozen North, Edward was developing an archaeological and environmental interest and a deep respect for "God's Country," as he called it.

Like our parents, my brothers Edward and Ted Liss contributed time and energy to organizations acting for the betterment of the Sangudo Community. That part of Alberta is a better place because of their many efforts.

In the years the Liss kids attended public school, the teachers were held in high esteem, any punishment given by the teacher was deemed to be appropriate. If we were ever strapped by our teacher and told our parents, they usually said, "You must have deserved it or you wouldn't have been punished." There were times when we didn't tell our parents if we realized we had deserved the teacher's strap. No child ever "told" on his siblings, we protected each other.

Our little schools, Poplar and West Cosmo had served our family well, taught us to respect our classmates, to do our best, and to take pride in our accomplishments.

Discipline, Country Style

The Liss Family - 1938

Sibling rivalry was a term I had never heard of until I took my first psychology course in High School. You were expected to look after your younger brothers and sisters and the oldest child was given permission to discipline his younger siblings if necessary. Our parents punished us if we were naughty, praised us when we deserved it and managed to make us feel loved, needed and secure.

Punishment, when we deserved it, was meted out by either of our parents. Mother's usually consisted of a smart handslap across our bottom but Father used a variety of more subtle methods.

If he ever walked in to find us quarrelling, he would tell us to embrace and kiss. If we were naughty, he pointed to the corner. "Klenchich!" "Kneel!" he commanded. He specified the number of minutes we were to remain by the degree of our misbehavior, three minutes for disobeying, five for a forgotten chore. We had to watch the clock and count the slow moving minutes. If we were noisy when he wanted to concentrate, he ordered us to run around the house several times. This punishment was reserved for wintery days and the thought of the sub-zero cold outside usually quieted us.

For really serious misbehavior, Father decreed a switching. The offending child would be sent to cut a switch suitable for Father to use. Whenever I was sent to find one I sobbed loudly all the way, procrastinating as long as I dared. Father would take the switch I reluctantly handed him.

"Now, how many switches do you think you deserve?" he asked fingering the branch.

I cried more loudly than ever.

"Do you know you have been bad?" he asked.

I continued to sob and nodded wordlessly.

"Are you sorry?"

More sobs and a nod.

"Will you try to be better?"

I nodded again.

"Very well," Father said sternly. "This time I won't use the switch. However, I shall put it over the door where it will be readily available if we ever need it again."

The twig hung there unused, until it shriveled, dried up and fell to the floor in brittle pieces.

I remember being spanked only once and that was when I was ten years old.

We had a rigid rule in our family that no matter where we were, we children were to be home before the sun went down. One Sunday I had spent the afternoon visiting neighbors two miles away. At five o'clock the lady asked,

"Don't you think you should be going home, Helen?"

"No," I replied. "Our parents let us stay out as long as we want."

"Oh?" she said. "Well, I suppose you are old enough to judge."

It was dusk when I walked into the farmyard where Mother and Dad were building a granary. Father looked up and saw me, put down his hammer, picked me up, turned me over his knee and spanked me soundly. Mother watched and never said a word.

"The sun went down an hour ago, young lady. See that this never happens again."

I was never late again and today, seventy years later, I recall that

Sunday evening with vivid clarity.

Our dad had a volatile temper that exhibited itself whenever machinery broke down and he had trouble making repairs. I remember him swearing in English and Polish. If we kids ever left a gate open and the cattle got into our garden, he exploded.

"SAC-ARA-MENTO!"

We all thought it was the worst swear word of all. Not until I was in public school did I realize Sacramento was the name of a city in California.

The responsibility our father carried on his shoulders was immense, always too much work, never enough money, always exhausted at day's end, no wonder his temper was sometimes short. "Your father works very hard," Mother would often say. Indeed he did!

One morning I heard a loud ruckus outside. Dad was shouting in anger.

"You kids stay inside," Mother ordered and we didn't dare ask why. Not until several days later did I learn what had happened. My two older brothers, Stanley and Vlad slept upstairs in the north bedroom. When time came to respond to nature's call, rather than use the pots we all had under our beds or traipse outside to the outhouse, both boys had urinated from the upstairs window. When Dad saw the yellow stains on the white walls, there was hell to pay.

Our Animal Farm

The early homesteaders were very dependent upon their animals, a good milking cow and a reliable team of horses often meant the difference between a farmer's success or failure. When John Liss and his father began homesteading in 1916, a cow cost $35.00 to $45.00 and a strong work horse sold for $200.00, costly investments for a beginning settler. Each homesteader tried to increase his herd by carefully breeding all his animals to produce young in the spring.

In his early farming days, Dad had to take his cows to a farmer who owned a bull, but within a few years, he was able to purchase his own, a pure-bred Short Horn bull. When neighbors brought their cows for breeding, Dad charged them $1.00 per animal.

One Sunday, Dad took a sow to a neighbors to be bred and the neighbor's wife scolded him.

"Shame on you Mr. Liss. This is the Lord's day, not a time for such things."

Once a year a stallion would visit our farm, trotting regally, led by his owner on horseback. That stallion was a splendid looking animal who sired many of Dad's dependable work horses.

As the years went by, Dad was able to increase his herds and add to his farm buildings. Gradually, he built a cow barn with stanchions, a big horse barn with a hay loft, a sheep barn, two chicken coops and several pig houses. Those buildings together with a huge granary and several machine sheds made an impressive, orderly looking farmstead.

We children were taught to never completely trust the animals, they could be unpredictable no matter how well they were treated. At one time or another, all of us had been butted by a ram or chased by an aggressive rooster. But it was the big bull we were afraid of. He would paw the ground, snort, then rush toward us. Even though a fence separated us, it was unsettling. Dad made a metal mask and fastened it to the bull's horns to limit his vision, but the crafty animal would toss the mask up over his neck and rush forward, unimpeded and angry. Dad then permanently fastened the mask to the bull's nose-ring so he could no longer fling it out of the way and we all felt safer.

Our Short Horn bull created an unpleasant situation with one of our neighbors. That neighbor was raising pure-bred cattle from his expensive registered bull, a different breed than Dad's Short Horn. He owned the quarter section adjacent to the field where Dad permanently pastured our bull. One spring the neighbor brought several young heifers to graze on his quarter, wanting to fatten them up before breeding them to his own registered bull.

When Dad's bull sensed the newly arrived heifers, he did what nature created bulls to do – he jumped the fence and impregnated all the neighbor's heifers.

The neighbor was furious – his breeding program was now set back a year – he lodged a complaint against John Liss with the R.C.M.P. The officer investigated and concluded there was no blame on our Dad's part. His report said Dad's bull had been in his field before the heifers were brought next door and every farmer should know a bull will go to any lengths to reach young heifers. No fence is high enough to keep him from trying.

Our farm always had numerous cats, the highest praise given to a cat was that she was "a good mouser". Cats were never allowed in the house except when a cat was expecting kittens. Then she could stay under the kitchen stove with her litter. We children eagerly watched to see when the little kittens would finally open their eyes, a miracle, we thought.

Our dogs were faithful and protective. If a dog was Valeria or Johnnie's pet, no one could abuse them – the dog would growl and act menacing. One time Dad fell down and when Mother tried to help him up, Dad's dog refused to let her come near him.

Our dogs kept the coyotes away from the farm animals. Whenever a faithful Rover died, it was a sad time for us kids, but we always got another dog and loved him just as much.

We had a hired man, a bachelor, Steve Heintz, whom Mother and Dad trusted and respected. They often left Mr. Heintz in charge of us kids if they had to be away. I never liked him because he once spanked me for something I felt I did not deserve and when I told Mother, she said,

"If Steve Heintz spanked you, you must have deserved it." I didn't, and I was indignant and unforgiving.

At the end of each month, Dad would write a check to Steve Heintz from his account at the Imperial Bank of Canada, Sangudo Branch. When I saw the amount, $25.00 I realized that was $1.00 per day wages. "What a lot of money," I thought. "Will I ever be able to earn that much cash?"

In the spring, when Saturday's work was done for the week, Mr. Heintz would borrow Dad's team of four work horses. He had no horses of his own so Dad lent Steve his horses so the man could put in his crop. As the horses and Steve disappeared up our hill, my Dad's comment was, "If it was anyone but Steve Heintz I would not commit my horses to work on a Sunday. Horses need a day of rest too."

My comment was, "Good! Mr. Heintz won't be here for supper and I'll have one less plate to wash."

We had a neighbor whom Dad disliked, in fact, despised. Since we got along with all of our neighbors, I could not understand my father's strong feelings against this one person. One day I asked him why he scorned Charlie.

"Helena, I find it almost impossible to be near that despicable man. This is what happened years ago. I was walking across The Flats near the Paddle River when I heard a terrifying sound. It was not anything I could recognize but a little like an animal moaning in agony. As I approached the sound became louder, shriller and more pitiful. Then I saw the cause. A work horse was tied to a post, and that neighbor was mercilessly beating the poor animal with a metal chain. It took all my self-control to keep from hitting that cruel man but I knew the R.C.M.P. would charge me with assault if I did so.

To this day I cannot forget the sound of that horse's pain nor can I stand to be near that contemptible man."

Faithful Old Kate

as told by John Liss

This is principally about our faithful old horse, "Kate". Before I start telling you about her, I must mention "Pete", a French Canadian horse which we lost under sad circumstances. The French Canadian horse was a breed rare in the West. Pete was big, all muscle and strength and always willing to work. Mosquitoes and flies were very nasty that summer on our homestead, so father covered Pete and the other horse, Jim, with horse blankets and let them out to graze.

There was an abundance of fine vetch and pea vine in those days. Unfortunately, there was a brush fire creeping slowly along the bush. Pete got too close to it and the blanket caught fire. He galloped in distress toward the cabin whinnying and calling for help. Father ran out and pulled the blanket off but it was too late. Part of Pete's rump was scorched and the damage was done.

I was in Calgary at the time winding up the office in preparation for enlistment. When father wrote to me about Pete, I went to a veterinarian who prescribed an ointment which I sent to father. For a couple of months, father dutifully tended Pete. Unfortunately, every time the scar healed up, Pete would bite into the proud flesh and tear it away. Father tried everything possible to prevent Pete from getting at the itchy spot, but to no avail. Eventually, infection set in and there was no other way out. There was no veterinarian in the district and so with a heavy heart, my father had poor Pete destroyed.

That meant that another horse had to be bought. Jim was only a saddle pony and a willing worker once you caught him, but also crafty, sneaky and hard to catch. By that time I was in the East training for the Army. Father went to Edmonton and at the Market Place spotted a young filly under two years. She was part Percheron, sorrel in color, well built and seemed to be of a good disposition. Father liked her and after hard bargaining, he bought her.

It took two days to walk home with her over the winding Lac St.

Anne Trail. Father was very fond and proud of the young filly and she seemed to respond to his care and caress. When she got older, he decided to break her into work. There was approximately a quarter of an acre of potatoes to cultivate, so father hitched Kate to the cultivator and tried to get her to work. To his disappointment, she absolutely refused. He tried every means of gentle persuasion, but it did not work. Kate would stamp her feet and shake her head; even a slender willow switch would not work. Finally, Kate laid down and appeared to say to father, "Now what are you going to do about it?"

As father was not versed in horse psychology, he was both worried and bitterly disappointed. There was a strong stout saskatoon in the bushes close by, so he cut it down, approached Kate and threatened her but she did not care. With the patch of potatoes to cultivate and a lovely young filly that refused to work, father was desperate. He decided that something drastic had to be done, and accordingly lashed with the saskatoon switch the full length of Kate's body. Kate looked at father in seeming dismay, got up, started to pull the cultivator and did a good job of it. Kate must have realized the romance was over and since then was a most reliable and faithful worker on the farm. Father would put a cowbell around her neck and let her out to graze. (There were no fences in those days.) If she was within hearing when he called, Kate would trot home and be ready for work.

By and by, I came home and started farming. Eventually, we bought a binder and my wife drove the four horses, one of which was Kate. Kate was very foxy and quite easy on herself. She always tried to ride the double tree and often had to be prodded on with a good bamboo whip. Meanwhile, I stooked the grain as that part of the job was rather hard on my wife. Our little infant was usually safely wrapped up in a sturdy box nearby, guarded by a faithful collie dog.

As time went on, Kate produced several fine foals. Later as she grew older, the children loved to ride on her "bareback" to school, 3½ miles away by road. Sometimes, 4 of them got on her back as she patiently plodded along. At the school grounds they would let her out to graze. At first, they hobbled her but later they found that Kate would stay close by awaiting for the children to be let out of school. The children were very good to her. They always brought a measure of oats to give her at noon and she used to consume all the left-over sandwiches given to her by our children and others. By that time, we had some good producing crabapple trees and the children used to fill their pockets. What they did not eat, they gave to Kate and she was very fond of them.

As Kate got older, she developed a growth on her knee and had a pronounced limp. In time, conditions and customs changed. Farmers began substituting tractors for horses and began to ship their horses to slaughterhouses. Under no circumstances would I allow our Kate to be sent away. There was another faithful old mare that I was very fond of and I turned both of them to the pasture on the new homestead. Kate eventually died at 33 years, a real old age for a horse. Yes, I will always remember Kate very fondly and I hope our children who rode her will also remember.

The seven Liss children and Kate - 1939

A final word on Kate:

When Kate was put out to pasture, she would come back to the barnyard every few days for a drink of water, stay for a while and then go back to the pasture. One Sunday, she did not leave, but took her drink of water and stayed in the yard. I had the boys catch and bridle her and bring her to the house yard. I took a picture of her with the five younger children on her back. First Helen, who was about twelve years of age and proudly wearing her first pair of white shoes, then Edward in front of her, next Teddy and Valeria, finally Johnny, 2 years old, almost sitting on Kate's neck. Altogether there were five children on her back with Stanley and Vlad standing alongside.

After the picture was taken, Kate was turned loose. She went through the yard gate into the barnyard and started for the pasture.

As she came to the turn in the pasture run, she stopped and looked back at the house. With all the family watching her, she stood for a few minutes and then slowly plodded away. Although we never saw Kate alive again, we will always think of her action as a last goodbye.

Mary Fridel's Sad Memories
And a few Smiles

What seems like cruelty in 2005 may have been an only choice 90 years ago. Mother told us a sad story from her early childhood that haunted her all her life. As a young girl, she had gone with her parents to visit a neighbor. When they entered the neighbor's tiny house Mary was startled to see a cage in the corner of the shack. Inside was a young girl making strange unintelligible sounds and agitated movements. Our mother told us she was bewildered and baffled and very disturbed.

In adulthood, Mother realized the neighbors had a mentally defective child and did not have the money to send her to the city to an institution. In those early days, there was no agency in Northern Alberta to assist them. What they had done was the only way the poor hapless parents could protect and care for their unfortunate child.

Another sad story was told to Mother by a woman about Mother's age.

The woman said as a child, she, her young brother and their parents lived in an isolated area of Northern Alberta, far from any neighbors. Every winter, the father left his wife and two young children alone in their cabin while he went off to look for work. In the middle of the winter the young boy died of a sudden illness. The mother was beside herself – she had no neighbors to turn to, no way to contact her husband. She could not dig a grave in the frozen ground, she had to put the body where animals could not find it and she did not want her daughter to see her brother dead.

When the little girl was asleep the mother laid her child's body on a slab of lumber in a shed, carefully sealing the door from predators. But the little girl, the one telling Mother the story, awoke asking for her brother. She missed her playmate and constantly kept asking her mother where he was. Each day she searched for him.

One day she found the body in the shed and rushed up to her mother.

"Mother! Mother! I found my brother. He is sleeping in the shed."

The woman telling our mother the story said her mother screamed and screamed and screamed. The poor mother could not stop sobbing, as the little girl clung to her.

But mother also told us about an amusing little incident that happened when she was working for a neighbor as a hired girl. The farmer, Charlie, walked in at noon with his hired man, Joe. After the meal, both men went into the living room and sat down in the upholstered chairs.

"Oh, Charlie," his wife said, "You are sitting on my best pillow."

Charlie obligingly moved to another chair.

"Oh, Charlie. That's my second best pillow."

Charlie got up, turned to his hired man and sighed. "Come on Joe. Let's go out and sit in the hay loft where there are no pillows."

Our Dad would often surprise us with a witty comment. I had sewn a white jacket for myself and was asking family and friends to sign their autographs on the cloth so I could embroider their names as a permanent souvenir. When I asked Dad to write his name on my jacket, he wrote, "Bill Payer."

When Mother saw what he had written, she said, "Well if your Dad is the bill payer, then I am certainly the Assistant Bill Payer."

Mother had a quick wit and a sense of humor that often emerged when she wasn't "dead tired."

When a new family moved in on the Paddle Valley Flats, it was months before Mother and Dad could take time from the pressing farm work to welcome their new neighbors into the district.

The two families eventually met and enjoyed a pleasant visit.

As our parents prepared to leave, Mother smiled at her new friend.

"We are so glad to have met you," she said. "And now that we have broken the ice, let's keep the water flowing."

One time Mother surprised us all by telling us this joke, where she heard it we never knew.

Two men took their reserved seats for a baseball game, congratulating themselves on their choice of such excellent viewing positions. A few minutes before the game was about to start, two Catholic sisters in full habitat seated themselves directly in front of the two men. Their wide wimples framed their faces and greatly restricted the view for the two men seated behind them.

"Oh, no!" one said. "Now I can't see. The next time I'm going to a ball game, it will be at the North Pole. They tell me there are no Catholics there."

His friend strained to look around the head-dress of the sister in front of him.

"The next time I go to a ball game it will be at the South Pole. They tell me there are no Catholics there."

One of the sisters turned around, looked at the two frustrated men and said,

"Why don't you two gentlemen go to Hell. There are no Catholics there."

Our Friendly Kitchen

In those cold Alberta winters, our house was a haven of warmth and security. It was always a relief to pull open the heavy storm door and step into a warm kitchen and undo all those heavy winter garments. Preparing the winter's supply of firewood for that essential warmth was an important fall task.

Dad cut trees on his new homestead and with a sleigh and team of horses, hauled the heavy poles into the back yard. He set up a noisy, smelly motor with a long wide belt that turned a big round saw. Then he and Stanley together lifted each heavy log up to the saw. Vlad grasped the cut piece of wood and deftly tossed it into a pile. Next those cut blocks had to be neatly piled against the well house wall and a pile of kindling needed to be chopped. Every Liss child knew how to use an ax. God forbid that we ever ran out of firewood.

When our Dad rebuilt the house after the 1928 fire he could not afford to insulate the house or build a foundation around the basement, consequently our house was very cold. Each fall Dad put up storm windows and doors, sealed off the front door entry and hauled a small stove into the living room for the duration of the winter. Over the stairway to our upstairs sleeping rooms, a heavy curtain was hung to keep the warm air downstairs.

My sister and I undressed in the living room around that little stove, then hurried upstairs to bed. The sheets were so cold, we huddled together to make a warm spot, but if you ever moved your body outside of that warm spot, frigid sheets shocked you awake.

Our kitchen was the friendliest room in the house. At one side was the bulky McLary stove with warming oven above, baking oven below and a hot water reservoir along the side. A long birch-wood table stood against a wall of the kitchen and around it the chairs and benches Dad had made.

Dad made all our furniture – benches, beds, chests, chairs from diamond willow with a willow couch to match. He made an exact rep-

71

lica of a Morris chair following instructions in a small blue book on carpentry. A farmer needed to be a carpenter, a mechanic, a blacksmith and a jack-of-all-trades. Our Dad was all of those; he had to be for us to survive.

When visitors came, they sat in the kitchen and we children sat quietly, listening attentively to all the neighborhood news and political discussions. What, I wondered were "parity prices"? I never did find out.

At last came glorious spring, the storm doors and windows came off, the door from the living room to the front porch was unsealed, down came the stairway curtain and out went the living room stove. Open doors and windows at last!

Later in the summer came the flies, flies by the hundreds bred in the barnyard and they all wanted inside our house. If there was a tiny hole in a screen, they found it. Flies covered the back screen door to the porch in a solid black sheet. We would grasp the screen handle, rapidly jerk the door back and forth, trying to dislodge some of the flies before we slipped inside. Sticky fly catchers hung from the ceiling of every room, but those persistent flies infiltrated throughout the house.

Every Saturday, Mother would cover all the food, hand us kids each a towel and take us upstairs to begin our fly eradication ritual. We waved towels to drive the flies ahead of us, down the stairs, into the living room and finally into the kitchen. Then Mother shut the kitchen doors and with a small flit gun, sprayed until dead flies fell on the kitchen floor. We hurriedly swept up the flies and burned them before they could revive.

When D.D.T. came, we suddenly had no more flies. It was a wonderful blessing for us until we sadly learned of the harmful effects of that chemical.

After a heavy snowfall the first path Dad dug was to the outhouse for our daily essential visit. Last year's Eaton's catalogue was our paper supply, but in below zero weather no one lingered to look at the pictures. We never did "freeze our buns off" because we hurried in and hurried out, back to the kitchen's warmth. In the summer, Mother planted flowers around the door of the outhouse and it looked quite pleasant amongst the native willows.

Our father was inquisitive, always eager to experiment with new ideas. One winter he sent for government pamphlets on how to tan animal skins. He studied, he deliberated, then decided to try his hand at being a tanner. If we thought the fermenting sauerkraut in the crock on the upstairs landing had a strong smell, it was nothing compared to Dad's crock of powerful tanning solution. What a disgusting smell each time we passed that putrid brew on our way to bed.

What Dad produced from this nauseating mix was surprisingly rewarding. Mother, Valeria and Helen benefited from warm fur wraps. Dad made Mother and Valeria lovely soft pairs of black and white mittens from rabbit fur and for me, he made a warm padded skunk-fur muff. Amazingly there was no skunk smell to my muff, only a soft fur to hold against my face in freezing winter temperature. I was very proud of my skunk muff – nobody in the countryside had ever seen one before.

Dad made all of our furniture with only basic hand tools. He had no power tools but with dedication and patience he created furniture that has been in use over 70 years. Our sturdy kitchen chairs were made of white spruce, the seats a smooth 2 foot wide slab of naturally blonde wood. The Liss family sat on those chairs for sixty years without a single one of them needing repairs.

One of our upstairs rooms became Dad's workshop. When I was a young child, I remember Mother walking up the stairs after supper, coal oil lamp in one hand, a baby on the other, we kids all traipsing behind her to see what Dad was working on. The room always smelled of spruce wood shavings – a nice smell. Dad's Aladdin lamp sizzled away casting a bright white light over his workbench as he proudly showed Mother his latest efforts.

"What is that furniture made of?" people would ask when they first walked into our living room. They were looking at chairs and tables made of willow, all a natural cream color with contrasting irregular shaped diamond indentations, of a crimson hue, a striking combination.

"That's our own unique diamond willow," Dad would reply.

If people were interested he went on to explain that diamond willow was really a Highland Willow that had been bruised when it was growing. If the bark had been broken by a fallen branch or by cattle or ice rubbing against it, the bruise healed over but inside a reddish diamond shape developed.

When Dad was tramping over his land, he always kept his eye open for bruised willows because he knew he would need a stock pile of at least 60 pieces to be able to select the 20 of just the right size that he would need to put together one chair. First he had to scrape away the rough, grey willow bark, then chisel out the pithy knobby areas that would become the reddish diamonds.

Each chair was painstakingly put together with holes, dowels and glue. He used no nails or screws. Dad sanded and hand-rubbed his creations for hours before he was satisfied. Only then did he paint on a coat of clear varnish.

I always wondered how it was that our Dad could explode in anger over some things but show infinite patience at other times.

Is it possible that seven growing children can at times be exasperating?

We all looked forward to those wonderful Saturday night baths. In late afternoon we began heating water on the wood stove, in the tea kettle, in pots and big pans, and carefully tended the roaring fire. Our long, thin tin bathtub was brought in from the back porch and installed in the middle of the kitchen floor. All doors to the kitchen were closed to keep in the warmth, the first kettle of water was poured in, then the kettle refilled and put back on the stove to reheat.

First to bathe was the youngest, little Johnnie, then after a fresh pot of warmed water was added, Valeria was bathed, another kettle of warm water added and Helen stepped in. Next the four boys bathed one at a time until finally all the family scrubbed, Mother had her welcome turn. Dad always bathed last. When the girls were bathing, no brothers were allowed in the kitchen and when the boys bathed, the girls had been sent off to bed.

Sunday morning when the tub had to be emptied, bucket by bucket, a goodly amount of wash water had collected in our tin bathtub.

The pleasure of Saturday's fresh sheets on our beds, clean underwear with snug ribbing at the wrists and ankles – it all felt so good. By week's end our underwear would have stretched so that we had to lap it over at our ankles before we could pull on our socks.

When I first visited an aunt in the city of Edmonton, a bathtub seemed like the height of luxurious living. Hot water came out of a spout, and when you were all bathed, you pulled a plug and all the water drained out all by itself. A modern marvel.

The first time I flushed a toilet, I knew I had broken it. At first there was a loud swish of water, but the sound didn't stop – it kept on and on. Should I tell my aunt I had ruined her toilet? While I was deliberating what to do, the sound stopped. Maybe the toilet wasn't broken at all.

"Catch-all" was what our big back porch was. If you ever needed a nail, a screw, some binder twine or a piece of hay wire, the first place you looked was the old table in the corner, piled with miscellaneous "stuff" you might someday need. Along one wall, a supply of firewood and kindling was piled high and replenished every evening. In the winter, a half of a beef steer hung from the ceiling. We children would laboriously slice off a thin sliver of that frozen meat and fry it in bacon fat for a quick snack. Dad's honey extractor, Mother's washing machine, the big round butter churn and any piece of Dad's machinery that needed repairing – all found a spot on that back porch. Lined against one wall there was always a row of muddy rubber boots in various sizes. Two built-in closets held our heavy garments and work clothes. If there was no space for the copper boiler or tin bathtub, they got shoved under the corner catch-all table. Amazingly, among all this array of clothing and equipment there was space for two chairs where we could sit and watch the sunset on a warm day.

Inside the kitchen near the door Dad had built a wooden stand, a medicine cabinet and a support for a bucket of drinking water. According to age, one child would be assigned the task of pumping water to keep that bucket always full. Above the bucket, a metal dipper from which we all drank, hung from a heavy nail.

My job was to make sure the tea kettle that was kept atop the McClary stove was always full of water. When a kettle was new, I could tell by lifting it, but gradually our "hard" mineralized water covered the inside of the kettle with scales and it felt heavy even when it was empty.

If we got a hole in our tea kettle or one of our cooking pots, Dad searched the back porch table until he found two rivets of the right size to stopper-up the hole. If a bucket that didn't go on top of the stove developed a leak, we plugged it with a rag. When we lost the screw-on top for the coal oil can, we stuck a potato on the spout in place of the lost cap. Sometimes I would hear our Mother say to one of my brothers, "This is broken. See if you can fix it." No matter the problem, they usually solved it.

Food Preparation

Food preparation was a major part of a farm woman's life. In the spring as soon as the ground had thawed we began to prepare for the winter's supply by planting a big vegetable garden, lovingly tending and weeding the carrots, parsnips, rutabagas and big potato patch. If there was a drought, we hauled buckets of water from the well for our growing crop. If there was to be an early frost, we gathered old rags and covered our precious vegetables. Everyone came to admire a tomato that had actually ripened on the vine. Not until many years later were early ripening varieties developed.

In the fall, we harvested the results of our summer's efforts, carrying buckets of vegetables into the dark basement, potatoes in the big bin, carrots, beets and rutabagas in smaller bins covered in sand. In the center of it all, stood a portable kerosene stove that would be lit on cold winter nights to keep everything from freezing. On those really bitter cold nights we carried pails of water into the basement. If that water began to freeze we knew we had to get out the old rags and cover our precious spuds.

Our dad used to say, "My children have never been hungry." True, but we sure had some monotonous meals. During the winter, every day for dinner and supper we had potatoes and one vegetable. One long, cold winter we used up all our vegetables and worst of all – no potatoes. The chickens stopped laying eggs that bitter March and the cows had "dried up" so we had little milk. We ate bread fried in bacon grease for a month, hot, crusty and greasy, we thought it was delicious.

Dad's bees supplied us with honey and we always had bacon that dad had smoked and cured hanging in the basement. We brought up a slab, scraped off the mould, fried it and ate it without a second thought. We boiled raspberry canes for a tea and we dried and ground dandelion roots to make a "coffee".

The dandelions that people call a weed were a blessing to us. As the spring snows melted we searched for the green leaves to cook as spinach or chop for a salad. When we saw a stock of red push up through the snow we eagerly waited for the rhubarb to grow tall enough to cook. We boiled pigweed and young nettles for a delicious spinach taste and a treat from our repetitive winter fare.

In the summer we canned. And we canned and we canned some more; two quart jars and one quart jars of wild strawberries, saskatoons, cranberries, blueberries, gooseberries, pembinas and currants. It meant jelly for our school lunches and dessert for our winter suppers.

My sister, Valeria, my younger brothers and I would be sent out in the mornings to a berry patch to pick the wild fruits. Each of us had our own berry pail and it was a pleasant chore to sit in some quiet spot where you could hear the birds and forest sounds. But some years, those pesky mosquitoes were almost unbearable. We would cut a poplar tree branch, swish it across our face with one hand and try to pick berries with our other. Those insects were unrelenting.

"Why, oh, why did God make mosquitoes?" I asked Grandma Fridel.

I don't remember ever getting a satisfactory answer.

In the afternoons we canned the fresh berries we had picked. The kitchen got so hot on an August day. We built a fire in the kitchen stove, boiled the fruit in one pot and sterilized the jars, tops and lids in another. Steam filled the room and perspiration ran down our cheeks, but at the end of the day, we proudly lined up the filled jars on the kitchen floor. When they cooled we took them to the basement, lining them up on the shelves, pleased with our day's efforts.

Years later, Mother would often say, "If we had only had electric power and a deep freeze when you kids were growing up, how much easier food preparation would have been."

In the late fall, we butchered a beef animal that had been set aside for that purpose. My sister Valeria and I were told to remain in the house, while Dad, Mother and the boys gutted and hung the animal from a tripod. By the time we were allowed outside, Mother had wrapped the hanging carcass in a white sheet and was sewing it shut to keep out the blow flies. That night we ate sliced fried liver, a rare and delicious treat for us. The next morning, the carcass was hand-sawed into quarters and the pieces carried onto the kitchen table. All day long our parents worked in the kitchen cutting and sawing the beef; some to can, some to pickle, some to smoke and some to save as fresh meat. During the butchering process we ate in the dining room on the oak table Grandfather Pozarzyski had saved from the fire. We ate there only on Christmas and special occasions.

If the animal butchered was a pig, then our parents made sausage. The entrails were scraped clean, washed several times, turned inside out, rewashed, then pushed onto a sausage maker fastened to the meat grinder. As you turned the grinder handle, the intestines came off filled with fresh ground pork that would be smoked in a smokehouse and served with sauerkraut in the winter.

Sauerkraut was made in a big crock that stood on the landing at the head of the stairs. After we gathered in our cabbage crop in the fall, we saved the finest heads for salads, the rest was made into sauerkraut. We shredded the cabbage into the crock with a cabbage shredder. When there was about 4" of cabbage shredded into the crock, we crushed it with a heavy wooden mallet Dad had made. Lift! Drop! Lift! Drop! When cabbage juice covered the shreds, we added salt, then repeated the process until the crock was full. A wooden lid, weighted down with stones covered the cabbage until it fermented into delicious sauerkraut. But oh! Did it ever smell throughout the house!

We gathered mushrooms and dried them in the warming oven to add to vegetable soups. Our dad always inspected what we had picked to ensure the varieties were safe to eat and we wouldn't get poisoned.

In the fall flocks of migrating ducks would land on Dad's grain fields. Dad told the boys to shoot those voracious eaters before they destroyed his crop. Mother roasted the wild ducks but I was distressed to find buckshot in my mouthful of meat.

Because we had a plentiful supply of wild berries, Dad suggested Mother make wine. A small wine crock stood atop the wood box near the kitchen stove. Dad was very pleased with Mother's wine making.

"This is delicious wine, Mary."

When my two brothers, Stanley and Vlad became teenagers, they would slip into the kitchen when no one was around, help themselves to a glass of wine, then add water to bring the liquid up to its original level.

"Mary" Dad said shaking his head, "your wine isn't as good as it used to be. What are you doing differently?"

The MᶜCLary Stove

Poor Mother!

Every three days, Mother baked a batch of bread, big crusty loaves cut into thick slices for our school lunches and to accompany each meal. We never used a recipe, everything was done by feel. A huge blue granite bread pan stood atop the wood base cabinet next to the stove. We dumped in the flour, made a hole in the middle and poured in the starter, then enough water to make the dough "just right." In the winter, as family members came in from outside, it was,

"Close the door or the bread won't rise. Keep out the cold. Shut the door!"

Sometimes we had no bread for the noon meal so Mother would make "Bangs". She heated a pan of fat to boiling, we took a scoop of bread dough, stretched it between both hands and dropped it into the bubbling oil.

"Poof!", the dough puffed up, turned a golden brown and tasted crunchy and delicious with Dad's honey poured over it. It was a rare treat because our dad said too much fat wasn't good for us.

My job was to make sure there was a proper fire in the stove. When the oven dial on the McLary reached up to three, that was the correct temperature to pop the loaves into the oven. A damper on the chimney, a damper at the side and a damper in the front of the cook stove all had to be regulated. The bin where the wood ashes fell had to be emptied every other day and dumped onto the garden. If there ever was a wind, the ashes would blow back in my face unless I covered the bin with a newspaper. Once I used a newspaper Dad had not yet read and I learned never to do that again after he voiced his displeasure.

My friend Lucy's family bought their bread at the store and it came sliced, every slice just like the other. At first we kids thought "store bread" was great but we always felt hungry soon after eating.

"That's because it is all air," our dad said.

Mother worried that we didn't get our needed Vitamin C during the winter. We didn't know that potatoes, our staple diet were high in Vitamin C. Our dad lectured us on the importance of scraping and peeling our vegetables thinly.

"That's where all the nutrients are – just under the skin" he would tell us.

One day he walked into the kitchen and stopped by the slop pail, the bucket where we tossed our vegetable peelings and wash water to be emptied out each evening into the pig trough.

"Who peeled these potatoes?" he roared as he picked up a thick peeling from the slop bucket.

"I grow vegetables to feed vitamins to my children, not my pigs. Who peeled these potatoes?"

I had been in a hurry and my knife was dull and rather than peeling thinly, I had hastily hacked at those potatoes, but I did not speak up. Since most of the cooking was done by Mother and me, I'm sure Dad knew I was the offender. He made his impression and from that day to this, I am careful to thinly peel the potatoes.

When times got better our parents ordered baby chicks in the spring. A strong, big, flat cardboard box with holes along the sides arrived at the railroad station in Sangudo on a Friday evening, crowded with 100 little yellow balls of peeping fluff. We watched eagerly as they grew waiting for the time the chicks grew big enough to provide a meal for us. The pullets were kept as future laying hens and the roosters would become our Sunday fried chicken treat. Usually the older boys deftly chopped off the rooster's head, Johnnie cried if he had to do it. My chore was to boil a kettle of water, scald the bird and pull out the feathers. The most annoying task was pulling out all those little pin feathers. Mother showed me how to dress the chicken and disjoint it into neat pieces. No fried chicken I have ever eaten has had the delicious flavor of those tender pieces we looked forward to in the early spring.

Chimney fires were scary things. If green wood was burnt or if a fire consistently was burned slowly, creosote collected on the stove pipes. Every spring, Mother, Dad and my brothers took the stove pipes apart, hauled them outside and scraped them clean of the messy, black accumulated soot before reassembling them.

About 10' of black stove pipe ran from the cook stove to the built-in brick chimney. This brick chimney did not get cleaned every spring and the creosote built up. When the chimney caught fire, it roared and crackled with an intense heat, shot straight up in a red burst of flame. If it hadn't been so frightening, it would have been beautiful.

Auction Sales

Farming in our section of the province was a constant struggle, often disillusioning and discouraging. In the depression years, many families gave up in sorrow and disgust, turning to less precarious methods of earning a living. Only the stubborn carried on; our father was certainly one of those.

Whenever a rural family decided to quit farming they would announce a public auction sale. A bill of sale was posted weeks in advance listing everything on their farm to be sold to the highest bidder – the cattle and the horses, the harnesses and the wagons, the furniture and the dishes, the pigs and the chickens, the machinery and the equipment – everything from threshing machines to Mason jars. The lady of the farm always provided free coffee and sandwiches for the neighbors who came from miles around to observe, to bid and to buy. Farm sales were often heartbreaking affairs as the man saw his hopes and labors passing beneath the auctioneer's gavel and his wife cried for their years of lost efforts and broken dreams. The meager monies collected at the sales end hardly seemed a fair reward for so many years of toil.

Whenever Father went to a sale we always waited impatiently to see what he would bring home. It might be a high brass ornate bedstead, or an old phonograph with Caruso records or a wooden washstand with porcelain pitcher and bowl. Once he returned with a complete set of Encyclopedia Britannica published in 1898 and another time with a typewriter so old that we were amazed to see it could actually type. He surprised Mother with the remainder of a set of fine china that some young bride had lovingly brought from England. He gradually stocked his machine shed with essential tools and farming equipment and added animals to build his herd.

Of all the things Father brought home from a farm sale, the one we never appreciated was his flour mill. Since he had bought it, he had to use it, but the flour ground from his mill resulted in the doughiest, heaviest, greyest, most unpalatable bread imaginable. No matter how well Mother mixed and baked the loaves, we children could scarcely swallow the tasteless mass. At first Father praised the bread lavishly but we noticed that after a suitable period he stopped taking a second slice. It was a happy day for the family when he brought home a sack of flour from the village store and moved his flour mill to the farthest corner of the machine shed.

"I wish Valeria and I could have some decent furniture for our bedroom," I said to Father one morning as he was preparing to leave for an auction sale.

"Very well, my dear. I'll see what I can do."

The furniture was as good as bought! All day long I had visions of a tiny dressing table with pretty flounces and a matching little ruffled chair. At last we girls would finally have a modern bedroom.

Father was pleased when he returned. "Here," he said proudly, "is a real beauty. It's all solid hardwood with a flawless plate glass mirror." My eager face fell at the sight of the long brown chest with the elaborate brass handles and the great oval mirror on swiveling arms, not a bit like the furniture I'd admired in the latest Eaton's mail order catalogue. It required Father and my two oldest brothers to carry the heavy piece upstairs.

By morning I had decided what I would do to modernize that chest. The ornate brass handles would be replaced with round wooden knobs, the dark brown wood would be painted pink and the great oval mirror would be removed and hung lengthwise on the wall.

With more eagerness than ability I unscrewed, unglued, hacked, sawed, pounded, measured and struggled until finally many bent nails and bruised fingers later, the enormous mirror hung by a neat strand of securely tied binder twine from a single inconspicuous nail. I stood back proudly to admire the results.

The family was seated downstairs at supper when a loud crash was heard from my room. I rushed upstairs to see torn binder twine dangling from a bent nail and shattered plate glass in jagged pieces around the room.

To my amazement I was never scolded, or have I just forgotten?

Mother was very proud of two pieces she had purchased at sales, a square pink china soup tureen that had once belonged to a former premier of Alberta and a tall pewter tankard. Premier Sifton's pink bowl had been promised to my brother and Mother said that the pewter pitcher would be given to me when I married.

With a fourteen year old's idea of beauty, I looked at the sturdy two foot tankard, the dull lusterless sides topped by a high pointed lid, the heavy curved handle and the unadorned base.

"I wouldn't have that monstrosity in my house!" I declared. "Why, it won't even take a polish!" When I was much older and a bit wiser, I realized that Mother's pewter pitcher was really a very valuable antique. When I told Mother I had changed my mind and wanted it after all, she shook her head.

"No," she said, "I offered it to you once and you refused. Now it will go to someone who will appreciate it."

My own gentle, considerate loving mother had just dealt me a disillusioning blow. Eventually, she did give me the pewter pitcher, but only after 40 years of regretting a 14 year old's lack of appreciation of a treasured gift offer.

Wash Day

By the time I arrived at the Sangudo High School at 9:00 a.m. on Monday mornings, the lady living nearest the school already had her wash neatly hanging on her clothesline and I would think, "My poor mother has only now milked the cows and is starting to heat water on the kitchen stove to start her wash."

Two adults and seven children made a huge pile of sheets, towels, underwear and outer clothing, all this to be scrubbed on a scrub-board propped against a round metal washtub. Water had to be pumped, carried in by buckets, heated in a copper kettle, then the dirty wash water hauled out and dumped on the garden. Mother ran the clothes through a hand wringer, then hung them on a pulley clothes line, operated from the back porch. In the summer when we brought in the clothes, they smelled so fresh and good. In the winter, everything froze on the line, stiff and hard. We carefully carried in the frozen articles, draping them over chairs and the upstairs banisters to dry.

One memorable day, Father returned from an auction sale, proudly hauling a motor driven washing machine onto the back porch.

"This will make your life easier, Mary" he said as he showed her how to start the gas driven engine by stepping sharply on a pedal. We children watched fascinated as the paddles turned around and around inside the tub. But the next Monday when Mother reached to step on the pedal, no pedal. In fact, no motor. The whole engine had been removed. On Sunday, Vlad had hauled the motor to a pond back of the barn where he was building a motorized raft. After a few sharp words from our dad, he sheepishly hauled the motor back and re-attached it to the washing machine where it belonged.

In the early farm days, Mother made her own bars of laundry soap using lye and sheep tallow. It was strong, smelly and hard on one's hands. It was a great improvement when we could afford to buy big boxes of TIDE.

A chore I disliked was ironing, especially on a hot summer day when the wood stove had to be fired up to heat the flat irons. To test if an iron was hot enough, we wet our index finger, then deftly touched it to the iron to test the temperature. If it didn't sizzle, the iron wasn't hot enough.

Invariably just as I would be about done ironing a shirt, I would scorch a collar or cuff. I decided that's why those irons were called "sad irons," because that's how they made me feel.

One summer a visiting cousin from Toledo, Ohio walked into the kitchen with her electric iron.

"Where do I plug it in, Aunt Mary?" We kids all laughed because we didn't have any place to plug it in. She hadn't realized we had no electricity.

Trials and Tribulations, Accidents and Illness

How we survived all our cuts and infections without tetanus shots or antibiotics must be a tribute to our inherited good genes. As kids we liked to go barefoot, it felt so good to squish the mud through our toes, but we often stepped on a rusty nail with a resulting painful swelling and infection. Mother would prepare a poultice of oatmeal mush and we sat for 30 minutes soaking our infected foot in the gruel. Sometimes she filled a bucket with hot water and salt and we stuck our sore foot in that to draw out the impurities.

Dad had numerous mishaps and near misses. Twice he had very close calls while fording the Pembina River, once near the old bridge site before the ferry was built and once while distributing ballot boxes near Park Court. A fording spot that was safe last year could change to a dangerous swift current after the spring thaw. Both times Dad's life was saved by the good swimming of his quiet reliable team.

Another time, Dad was not so lucky. He was watering his horses when something terrified them and they bolted, knocking him down and tramping on his shoulder. He was unconscious when Mother found him and in severe pain as she led him into the house. Our dad suffered from arthritis for the rest of his life, due he thought to that accident.

For as long as I can remember, Dad had bees to fertilize his orchard and provide honey for his family. When he tended his bees, he was careful to don all his protective clothing and seldom got stung until one unforgettable day when hundreds of honey bees attacked him relentlessly. He ran through a hedge to dislodge them. It didn't stop them. He called for Mother, they attacked her, she called for Stanley and he was able to light a smudge pot and quiet the pugnacious insects.

It was the only time I remember my father being in bed for two days, unable to move. When he recovered, he was surprised to realize he had no arthritis pain and for two years after his bee-sting incident, he was pain free. Was there a relationship between the bee stings and the relief from arthritis?

In the early homesteading days, if a family contracted a communicable disease, a big yellow sign, "QUARANTINED. DO NOT ENTER" was tacked to the door of the house. When we all had measles, that sign was nailed to our back door. I felt as if we were untouchables.

When I was about eight years old, I developed a painful tooth ache. After the second day, as he watched me suffering, Dad said,

"I'll try to pull that annoying tooth and give this girl some relief."

He boiled a pair of pliers to disinfect them, and while Mother comforted me, he attempted to pull the offending tooth, but I would flinch in pain each time he tried.

"Mary, I just can't do this. We have to drive her to the dentist in Mayerthorpe."

The dentist gave me an anesthetic and to my intense relief, the pain went away. When I awoke, the tooth was out, I didn't hurt but I was so embarrassed. I had wet my pants!

In 1941, Dad was stationed in Edmonton at the Army Recruiting Office when Mother took a few days off to visit him, leaving Stanley, Vlad and Helen in charge of things. My two younger brothers, Edward 12 and Ted 10, had been sent to a gravel pit on "the new homestead" to bring a load of gravel back to the farm. They loaded up their two-wheeled cart and started for home. Coming down a short, steep hill, the gravel all slid to the front of the cart, the cart tongue broke, Edward was pitched forward and a cart wheel ran over his shoulder. By the time he got back to the farmhouse, he was in intense pain. Stanley and Vlad knew they had to get him to a hospital in Edmonton.

We phoned Mother where she was staying in Edmonton with Auntie Oly and she said,

"Take Edward to see Mrs. Langston before the boys start driving in. Auntie Oly and I will wait for them at the Royal Alec Hospital."

Mrs. Langston was a respected nurse, and now that we had no local doctor, she was the only medical professional in our community. We often came to her for help.

Mrs. Langston examined Edward and said he had a dislocated shoulder.

"Does it hurt badly?" she asked.

"No," Edward replied. But as he turned to walk away, he moaned in pain.

"Oh! Oh!" Mrs. Langston called out. "Come back."

She told Mother she gave Edward a pain pill, but Ed was probably in shock and remembers none of this.

Mother told us she and Auntie Oly waited 4 long hours before the boys finally arrived. She worried that there had been car trouble or an accident, the hours seemed to drag by so very slowly.

"No troubles," Stanley said "We had to drive carefully so we wouldn't jar Edward's shoulder, and we had never driven to the Royal Alec before so we didn't know exactly where it was."

All our milk cows were gentle, quiet animals except for one big white animal. She was "a good milker" and gave more of a richer milk than the others, so we kept her, but she was mean. One evening when Mother went out to milk, the white cow charged at her, picked Mother up between her horns and tossed her over the fence. The next day Stanley and Vlad drove the cow into a stanchion where they secured her head and sawed off her horns. Mother said,

"I was lucky she picked me up on her horns and did not gore me."

Vlad and I were home alone one afternoon when he walked into the kitchen holding his hand over his wrist, blood gushing out and running down his arm.

"Oh! My God! What happened?"

"Just be quiet and put a tourniquet on my arm. I have cut an artery while I was working in the machine shed."

We knew how to apply a tourniquet because we had been taught the process in public school. We twisted the cloth tight around Vlad's arm until the blood stopped flowing. I tore up tea towels and we wound them snugly over his wrist. When his arm began to turn white, we released the tourniquet, wound more bandages and eventually stemmed the flow. When Mother came home she instructed Vlad not to use that arm until it had healed.

Exactly one week later, Vlad came into the kitchen covering his bleeding wrist. "Oh no, not again," I shuddered.

"Helen! I was welding and I opened up my wound. Quick! Fill the wash basin with cold water."

We could not stem the flow and as the basin filled with red, I was afraid my brother would suffer from loss of blood. We were desperate.

"Get me a handful of flour."

Vlad held the flour over his cut hand and eventually sealed off the flow of blood. In time his wrist healed with no after effects.

When my sister Valeria was born I was delighted. At last, after four brothers, I would have a companion, a girl to keep me company. At six years of age my earliest memories of Valeria are of embarrassment and helplessness. My sister had been born in the Barrhead Hospital, a long, low building where the babies were kept in cribs near the entry. When baby Valeria was pointed out to me, I leaned over her crib murmuring to her and praising her beauty. Next day when we again came to visit, I walked over to the same crib and again admired and cooed with my new sister. Then the nurse came by and told me Valeria had been moved to another crib and I was admiring a stranger. I was an embarrassed six year old.

In the early 1930's doctors advocated feeding babies only at specified times. Valeria would cry and cry and I felt so helpless holding my sobbing sister. Then Mother decided Valeria was crying only because she was hungry, so she dropped the specific feeding time rule and all went well, no more crying sister.

Dad said he would watch little Valeria walking home from Cosmo school, so weary and slow, always the last one home.

"Mary, we have to take that child into Edmonton and have her examined. Something is not right." Something was indeed wrong. When she was examined, the doctors found she had an overactive thyroid, a heartbeat of 130 and that she needed an operation when she reached girlhood. Our parents made her a bed in the dining room so she would not have to climb stairs and for a year she lay quietly downstairs on her cot. We were all admonished never to upset or tease her. Years later, Valeria recovered and grew into a confident young lady, but always "my little sister."

John Robert

"Helen raised Johnnie," Dad used to say. I believed him until I had kids of my own and realized that his statement was a bit of an exaggeration.

There always seemed to be a baby in our house. After me came Edward, then Ted, Little Sister Valeria and then Baby Johnnie. When Johnnie was born in 1935 in the Barrhead hospital I was eight years old and felt he was a gift just for me. He was a good-natured child, never cried, smiled when we talked to him and laughed when we held him. The day he was one year old, he took his first hesitant steps from the stove to the cream separator. We all clapped and he laughed, pleased with his accomplishment.

Whenever Mother left the house to do evening chores, I would sit in Dad's diamond willow rocking chair, holding Johnnie and singing to him. With Mother absent the house slowly got dark and seemed cold and lonesome, yet as soon as Mother entered the house with her milk pails, her very presence seemed to warm the room.

She emptied her milk pails into the cream separator, put more wood into the kitchen stove and reached for the coal oil lamp . Every evening she blew on the globe, rubbed it with a newspaper until it shone, turned up the cotton wick, trimmed off the ragged brown tip and struck a match to light our only kitchen lamp. Now that the house had a warm fire, a yellow lamp light and Mother in the kitchen, it didn't feel lonesome any more.

My evening chore was to wash the supper dishes. One evening when I put Johnnie to bed, I stayed and sang to him. I thought "If I stay here long enough, maybe someone will do the dishes," so I stayed and sang some more. Half an hour later when I walked back into the kitchen, there were the dirty dishes, still on the table, still waiting to be washed. I was indignant!

I took great pride in watching my baby brother grow and I knew I was personally responsible for his agreeable nature and pleasant disposition. I had never heard of "genes!"

In the summer of 1941, a car drove into our yard. People we did not recognize walked up to our back door.

"Can anyone tell us how to get to Barrhead?" they asked.

Barrhead was a town 35 miles northeast of our homestead. Our roads had no highway numbers and no names except the unofficial names we farmers gave them, names like The Lake Romeo Road, Horseradish Corners, Kelly Mutton's Hill, the Big Rock with "Jesus Saves" painted on it, Skunk Hollow, The Meadowview Store Road – all known to us locals but meaningless to an outsider. It was impossible to give directions to a stranger on how to get to Barrhead.

As Mother and Dad chatted with the strangers they learned the couple were members of Dad's political party, the C.C.F. (Co-operative Commonwealth Federation). They were friends of active C.C.F.'ers our parents knew and were on their way to a political rally in Barrhead.

Mother and Dad decided 6 year old Johnnie would go with the couple and guide them to Barrhead. They were to drop him off at Grandma Fridels where his sister, 8 year old Valeria was spending the summer.

Valeria said when the stranger's car drove into Grandma's yard, Johnnie hopped out of the car and came up to her smiling.

"I only made one mistake," he proudly said. "I only made one wrong turn."

Pretty good for a six year old, we all thought.

Whenever someone in our family had a birthday, we always baked that special person a birthday cake, carefully putting a big button and a big penny into the layers. If your slice of cake had the lucky penny, you would grow up to be rich. There was great laughter when some-one got the button.

"Ha! Ha! You are going to be an old maid. Ha! Ha!"

When Johnnie got the button, he asked, "Can I trade this button for the penny? I'd rather be rich than be an old maid."

John had an impish streak and a knack for little jokes. One after-noon I heard him snickering as he read our local paper, the Lac Ste Anne Chronicle. He and Valeria had written a made-up letter to an advice column and the paper had printed it with an appropriate reply, not realizing that two mischievous kids had engaged in a bit of tom-foolery.

The Liss Library

In 1922 when our parents were married the railroad had reached Sangudo only seven years before in 1915. The rail line terminated at Whitecourt, forty miles west, that was "the end of steel."

Our little hamlet had a hotel, a post office, store, livery stable and various small businesses. Sangudo's sidewalk were wooden planks that would flip up and hit you if you didn't walk carefully in the middle. But it was crossing the street to get to a business on the other side that was a real challenge. The sticky, heavy gumbo clung to our boots as we tried to navigate the muck without leaving a shoe behind.

By 1937 Sangudo became large enough to be incorporated as a village. A passenger train came from Whitecourt twice a week every Tuesday and Friday at 9:00 A.M., carrying passengers to Edmonton, 80 miles away. At 8:00 P.M. in the evening the train returned, stopping for water at a huge tank east of the platform. We kids liked to jump on the train at the water tower and ride the short distance to the station platform whenever we happened to be in town. The conductors never scolded us. They knew it was the only train ride most of us ever had.

Trips to Edmonton were a rarity, necessitated by illness or pressing business. We children would never forget the time our dad returned from the city with a memorable surprise – a huge box full of books. The Edmonton Library had sold their worn books for pennies a book. Such wonderful titles, "Riders of the Purple Sage," "The Call of the Wild," "Tarzan of the Apes." Vlad picked "All Quiet on the Western Front" and occasionally snickered as he read his book. Dad wanted me to read "The History of Mankind" but I picked the mysteries, "The Blue Hand", and the "Insidious Dr. Fo Man Choo" captivated me. We lent books to our neighbors, everyone got pleasure from our library. Dad built a 6 foot long bookcase to hold our newly acquired treasures.

One of our neighbors was Frankie Mason, the son of Mrs. Harris. Frankie always had a lonesome look to him and when Dad offered to lend him some of our books, Frankie was pleased. On his next visit, he wanted to reciprocate and brought us some of his reading material. When Dad saw what it was, "True Confessions" and various Pulp Magazines, he said,

"My children aren't reading this trash," and he stashed the magazines at the bottom of the wood box, piled wood over them and tore pages off as fire starter. When no one was around, I would dig out a True Confessions magazine and guiltily read the lurid accounts. Lucky for me my parents never caught me!

Lucy, my high school buddy read a lot and knew big words I had never heard of. She would ride home with me from High School perched on the handlebars of my bike. One day, passing the Hodges place, she said,

"Those boys are illegitimate, aren't they?" I had never heard the word, but I couldn't let Lucy know so I said, "Oh, well, I'm not sure of that."

When I got home I asked Dad,

"What does illegitimate mean?"

He put his newspaper down and asked,

"Where did you hear the word?"

"Lucy said the Hodges boys are all illegitimates."

"Well, my dear, let me explain. Mrs. Hodges was a widow and needed a job, so she became Major Garrity's housekeeper. Major Garrity had a wife in England but she refused to come to Canada. A man needs a women and so over the years Mrs. Hodges and Major Garrity have lived together and had several children. Major Garrity can't marry her because legally he is still married."

He paused for a moment then said,

"My dear, circumstances alter cases."

A much publicized book came out about 1938 called "Gone With the Wind." We coaxed our parents to get it for us, finally Mother was able to save enough to buy a paperback. That winter we all took turns reading the thick book by the light from a new gas lamp. Each evening, Dad would pour white gas into the lamp's round metal base, pump air into it with a small pump, screw the cap on tightly, then light the mantle. The lamp gave off a brilliant white light as it sizzled hanging from a hook in the ceiling. We lent our new paperback to a friend, she lent it to her friend, and when we eventually had "Gone With the Wind" returned to us four months later, the last three pages were missing.

One of the magazines we always had in our house was McLeans, a Canadian publication with timely articles on a wide variety of subjects. One afternoon two strangers drove into our yard, announcing they were selling McLeans subscriptions. As the men got out of the car, our two dogs, Baldy and Rover began to bark, and they barked and barked. One man was on crutches because he had only one leg. The dogs seemed especially agitated by him. No matter how we scolded those two dogs, we could not stop their incessant barking and they refused to be shooed away.

Mother felt sorry for the one-legged man and even though her subscription had not yet expired, she paid him for another year's issues. Not until the men drove off did Baldy and Rover calm down.

In a few weeks Mother got a letter form McLean's Magazine warning people that two con men were posing as legitimate agents for the publication and not to give them any money. If a subscriber had already given these two con men money in good faith, McLeans would honor a six month subscription.

When we read that letter, we were all convinced that Baldy and Rover sensed the insincerity of those two con men and were trying to convey that to us by their angry barking.

Our dad had not had a formal education, only a few years in a Russian school and some schooling in Toledo. But he had a curious, inquiring mind. He read. He remembered. He questioned. He carried a dictionary and checked every unfamiliar word. He read his newspaper at the supper table, propping it up against the milk pitcher. Tired as he was, he found the energy to read a few minutes every evening after supper.

When he read something with which he strongly disagreed, or if he felt something was unfair or incorrect, he wrote letters. I remember him on rainy days sitting at the dining room table, pencil and paper next to his dictionary. He wrote and rewrote. When he was satisfied, he asked Mother to read it and give her opinion.

Then he used precious carbon paper and wrote his final draft and filed away the carbon copy. He letters were articulate, accurate and well-written as exemplified by this reply to incorrect information on Red Fife Wheat.

The Incorrect Information

Canada's debt to Russia

Sir: What does Western Canada owe to Russia? Red Fife wheat for one thing. The story of how Red Fife wheat came to Western Canada is too well known to need repeating. Red Fife wheat put the western farming country on the map as the world's best soil and climate to grow the wheat that made the world's top flour for bread making.

Brome Grass was first called "Austrian Brome" because the first seed used in Western Canada came from Austria. But the Imperial Russian agricultural scientists gave the seed to the Austrians. The trees best suited to prairie conditions are natives of Russian prairies or steppes – Russian poplars and Russian willows.

An exchange of scientific knowledge about production of food plants makes for world peace.

-Gordon McLaren, Pipestone, Man.

The Correct Version

The origin of Red Fife wheat

Sir: This is in reply to Mr. Gordon McLaren, Pipestone, Manitoba re the Canadian debt to Russia. He mentions that Red Fife wheat came from Russia. I wonder by what process of mental gymnastics he came to that conclusion.

The wheat from which that sample came was loaded aboard ship at the Baltic port of Gdansk (then known as Dantzig) under German control. Before it arrived at Gdansk, it was loaded on to lighters and floated down the Vistula River or one of its tributaries. All of that hinterland up to the Carpathians was part of Poland, some of it was controlled by the Germans, and some by the Austrians, but mostly by the Russians.

The only Russians living there were the army garrisons, and officials, whose purpose was to hold Poland under control. Poland was then a grain exporting nation, the land was owned and worked by the Poles. It was rather fortunate that a sample of that wheat family got to David Fife in Canada, and lucky that his cow did not gobble it all up in his garden! Anyway, it multiplied and produced the crops on our prairies, and, later by cross-breeding by scientists like Dr. Saunders it was improved to Marquis quality. Most of our modern wheats have at least some of the Red Fife strain.

No Mr. McLaren, Red Fife did not originate in Russia. Lagoda and perhaps other varieties did. The famous winter wheat, Kharkov came to us from Ukraine.

Let's give credit where credit is due.

- John Liss, Sangudo,

Fun and Games

Even though we had never ending work, we still had time for fun. In the long winter evenings, we all read or we listened to Mother read to us. We made things, we did embroidery work, we sewed, the boys worked with wood or made baskets from willows and birch bark. Our family was big enough that we could always find someone who wanted to play together at dominoes or snakes and ladders. If we started a game of Monopoly it often lasted until midnight, with animated laughter and playful threats.

When we were little, we played "store" under the big maple trees between the house and the barn. I told my younger siblings I would be the store-keeper because I was the oldest of the group. Ed, Ted, Val and John had to line up to buy things, but everything we had for sale was make-believe. However, our money was real, thick round slices of white turnip which we would eat when we tired of our game.

Behind the farm buildings a small stream meandered across our farm on its way to The Flats and the Paddle River. Where the stream had cut higher banks, a family of muskrats had built a muskrat house, partially damming our stream and creating a small pond. The pond wasn't very deep so we children were allowed to play in the water under the supervision of our two older brothers. Stanley and Vlad built a raft of small logs and would give us rides around the pond. It gave us many years of pleasure until one summer when we all came out of the water, our whole bodies covered in red raised welts about ½ inch long. Blood suckers had invaded our swimming hole and we could never swim there again.

One winter Stanley and Vlad made us a skating rink. They cordoned off one of the animal pens and began pumping water into it. When you have to pump water by hand for an hour to fill the big animal trough, that is work, but when you pump to make a skating rink, that is fun. Their rink was a big success where we played "Crack the Whip" and our own unique version of hockey.

One warm winter day Mother loaded us all into the farm sleigh with the big sleight box on top, and with lots of warm clothes and blankets we set off to visit the Salmon family, two miles east of us. Our trail took us along a steep sloping hillside. For some reason, our big farm sleigh tipped over, dumping Mother, children and blankets into a thick snow bank. Mother laughed. The team of horses stood patiently as we all scrambled up, shook off the snow, lifted the sleigh upright and continued on our journey.

On another winter day, a Sunday, Mother dressed us all in our best clothes and started off for Catholic service in Sangudo. It was a slow 4½ mile ride and by the time we got to the church, the service was over. The priest spoke to her.

"My child, God knows you came. God knows you tried to come on time."

Summer was a time for ball games and our favorite game of "Anti-I-Over." Half of us gathered on the east side of the house, half on the west side. The idea was for one team to throw the ball over our two story house, the other team was to catch the ball, sneak around and put their opponent "out." Unfortunately some of us couldn't throw the ball high enough and we often hit the dormer window, shattering the glass. Our chore was to clean up the broken glass, replace the pane and putty up the window. After several years we had a number of amateurishly puttied windows.

None of us will ever forget those wonderful winter dances in Cosmo School. Our whole family piled into the horse drawn sleigh, singing all the way, wonderful songs like "You are my Sunshine," "Good Night Irene," "Frankie and Johnny." When we arrived at the school, the desks had been pushed back, a gas lamp hung from the ceiling and the orchestra was in place. Talented local boys played the accordion, the guitar and the violin and everyone, children and adults danced. Families laid their sleeping babies across the desks, the ladies arranged the sandwiches and cakes they had brought for midnight lunch as laughter filled the room. No one cared if we square-danced according to the correct rules, we danced energetically for fun as the men "swung their partners round and round" with a vigor that frequently took our feet "off the ground."

Just before midnight supper, we held the Moonlight Dance. The teacher took the gas lamp down, carried it into the cloak room and closed the door. Now we could dance in the dark with our favorite partner as you held each other close. All too soon, the teacher carried the lamp back into the room.

To raise money for Cosmo School, a box social would be scheduled. Each young girl brought a box lunch to be auctioned off. She then had to have midnight supper with the person who bid the highest amount for her box lunch. We girls would give a hint to our favorite beau to make sure he would bid on our box. Sometimes two men would try to outbid each other for the same box and that was great fun as the crowd urged them on.

By 3:00 a.m. we were all bundled up for the trip home, still full of energy, still singing, "You are My Sunshine."

I liked to sing. I sang when I milked the cows. I sang when I picked berries. I sang when I did the housework. If there was a song that had a special appeal to me, I sang it over and over. One day I liked the sound of "Carry me back to Old Virginie" and sang it all morning long.

"Helen!" an exasperated Stanley said, "Aren't you there yet?"

Model T and Model A

Sometime in 1931, Dad bought his first car, a second-hand Model T. He bought it, not to replace our horse and wagon, but to have in an emergency. Such an emergency arose only a few months later.

In 1931, when I was 4 years old, I fell from a pile of lumber in the back yard. Mother said she saw Stanley leading me, my left arm below my elbow hanging down. She knew immediately what had happened and sent Stanley to get Uncle Frank a mile away. Vlad was sent to the field to alert Dad.

Dad hastily checked over the Model T, Mother put pillows onto the back seat and Uncle Frank sat down to support me. Soon we were off to see a doctor in Edmonton, 80 miles away.

Each time we hit a bump, I would moan in pain and Father would swear. The roads were rough and rutted. Once a car got into a deep rut, it was almost impassible to steer the car out. Dad got behind a farm truck operated by one of our neighbors, a cantankerous fellow whom he disliked. When Dad indicated he wanted to pass, the neighbor refused to pull over. Dad honked his horn and yelled "Emergency", but the fellow only laughed and slowed down. Not only did he slow down, he would stop abruptly, then drive on as slowly as he could. When miles later, the truck finally turned off onto a side trail, the driver laughed again. I remember my dad shaking his fist and yelling,

"You filthy Son-of-a-Bitch."

My only other memory is of the day my cast came off and how pleased I was to see my arm whole and well.

The Model T was not dependable. Something was always breaking, tires would go flat and it was "a bugger" to start. After a few years, Dad traded it in for a used Model A. Sometimes I would ask if we could drive somewhere in our new car and Dad would reply,

"No dear, We don't have a license."

We visit Grandmother Fridel in the Model "T" – 1935

How is it, I wondered, that you needed a license to make a car run?

An event we looked forward to was an annual drive to Grandmother Fridel's in Barrhead. Although it was only 35 miles away, poor roads and an unreliable car made for an uncertain trip that required days of preparation. Dad and the boys tinkered with the car, and loaded in our supplies, tire patches, a shovel, an ax and a rope. By 9:00 o'clock, chores all done, "us kids" scrubbed and clean, we and Uncle Frank piled into the Model A. The talk was of how many flat tires we would have and how many mud holes we'd encounter. One time the tire jack had been forgotten and Dad broke off several fence posts to jack up the car. The men patched the tires after each flat, pumped in the air, reassembled everything and we optimistically started off again.

Whenever we came to a mud hole, the men walked out to inspect the best way to drive through. Sometimes, they chopped poplar trees to lay across the mud, sometimes they tied a rope to the front of the car and the boys, Uncle Frank and Mother pulled the car as Dad drove slowly until the car reached drier ground. The worst spot of all on the road to Barrhead was Kelly Mutton's hill. A wet, soggy half mile stretch of road just before a steep hill defeated us every time. "I wonder," Mother said, "Will we ever make this trip without getting stuck and making it to the top of Kelly Mutton's hill?"

It would be about 12:30 when we finally arrived at Grandmother

Fridels. She always had a special meal for us, home-made pork and beans and canned chicken. No sooner had we eaten, than the men all went out to inspect and again tinker with the car. About 4:00 p.m., when they felt all was in order, it was time to start home. The chores were waiting and the cows had to be milked.

"I wonder" Grandmother would say, "if the time will ever come when John can sit and visit and not spend his time repairing that car?"

Shortly after Dad bought the Model A, he decided to give Mother driving lessons. I always thought the way he introduced her to driving was pretty stupid and dumb.

The Model A was kept in the well house, the same building that had been our home after the fire. This building was about 2 feet above ground level, so the car had to be carefully backed out along two narrow inclined planks. Backing the car down these two wooden ramps was Mother's first driving lesson. She stepped too heavily on the gas, the car bolted down, sped across the grass and slammed into the tall spruce pole that held our lightening rod, knocking it over.

Dad was furious! His temper flared and recriminations followed. When he finally calmed down, Mother said very quietly,

"I'll never drive a car again."

Not until 50 years later, after Dad had a stroke and was unable to drive, did she realize that she would be isolated on the farm unless she learned to drive, so at 70 years of age, she signed up for driving lessons.

When she graduated, the instructor said, "You are a good and careful driver, Mrs. Liss, in spite of what your husband will say." A comment probably based on the instructor's years of experience with husbands.

That Model A was the source of much pleasure to us. Sometimes on a hot 90° summer evening, chores all done, we would ask if we could go swimming in the Pembina River, 4 miles away. If the boys assured Mother that we had enough gas, we would run upstairs and hang a white sheet from the dormer window. That was the signal to my friend Amy, who lived ¾ of a mile west of us to join us for a swim. Neither of our families had a telephone but our communication system worked and soon Amy would come running. We all piled into the car, honked our horn in front of another neighbor, the Hodges boys and soon both running boards full, we noisily sang all the way to the river. Mother sat on the bank carefully watching us. It felt so exhilarating to swim in that clear river water; we drove home happy and refreshed.

At the top of the river hill not far from where we went swimming, lived a bachelor, Mr. Vod. Mr. Vod grew hemp – not marijuana, but hemp, we were told. When Dad asked him why he smoked the hemp he grew, Mr. Vod replied,

"It makes me feel good."

Our dad said, "The old gentleman lives alone, has no family and if smoking his hemp gives him pleasure, what difference does it make? He's not hurting anyone."

Vlad enjoyed the challenge of that Model A. Often he would be cranking the car, over and over with no results. I would be behind the wheel and Vlad would call out "Choke it! Choke it!" What a relief when the engine finally spluttered and roared into full power – such a beautiful sound to two frustrated anxious kids.

In the sub-zero cold winters, Vlad soaked a rag in gasoline, laid it across the manifold and carefully lit it. Flames shot up.

"Isn't that dangerous?" his worried sister fretted.

"I'm trying to warm up this cold metal so the engine will be easier to start." A guardian angel must have hovered over us because we never had an accident.

One Sunday when Vlad was 16, he asked our parents if he and I could go for a drive. They agreed so off we went. A short distance from the farm Vlad said, "Let's go to Barrhead and see Grandma."

"Oh no. We can't go all that way and be home by dark."

"Sure we can. Let's go for it." We felt mischevious, adventuresome and daring as we bounded along the 35 miles to Grandma's place. Everyone was surprised and pleased to see us. They fixed a big supper; we laughed and talked until I looked at the living room clock.

"Vlad! It's getting late. We have to head for home."

By the time we reached the barbed wire entrance gate to our farm it was indeed very late and very dark. Vlad turned off the car lights, so that in theory our parents would not see us returning home at this near midnight hour. We had left that wire gate open, but during our absence, someone had closed it. The car smacked into the closed gate with a crunching sound, followed by my brother's hopeless despair.

"Oh, my God! Are we in for trouble, Helen."

He turned off the motor and we coasted silently down the ¼ mile into our back yard. Next morning Vlad got up very early and repaired the barbed wire gate before anyone saw it. As for the front of the Model

A, there wasn't enough damage to draw attention to it. Our guardian angel was still with us.

Gasoline was cheaper and easier to obtain for farm trucks than for cars, so our Dad had toyed with the idea of converting the Model A into a farm truck. Vlad brought that idea to fruition. One Saturday, driving home from a dance, he was either going too fast, didn't have good brakes or had drunk too much dandelion wine when he rolled the car over, resulting in extensive damage to the rear end.

Dad would be furious. What was Vlad to do? He drove the car to the blacksmith shop in Sangudo and told the mechanic to convert the Model A to a farm truck A.S.A.P. Apparently, our Dad wasn't too upset when he saw the remodel.

One Saturday when we all went into town in our "new" truck, Mother saw a sign in the grocery store, "Special. Five cans of tomatoes - $1.00." Tomatoes were a real treat for us, so we all pooled our money and were able to come up with $1.00. We put the bag of tomatoes in the back of our truck but when we came back a few minutes later, the bag was gone. Someone had stolen our tomatoes, the first time that ever happened to us in Sangudo.

There were two prices for gasoline, one price for regular car gas and a lesser price for purple gas to be used only for running farm machinery. Farmers would put the cheaper purple gas into their automobiles, but if the R.C.M.P. ever stopped them and found the colored gas in their tank, the unhappy farmer would be heavily fined.

Vlad decided there must be a way to neutralize the purple color of the gasoline. Saturday after Saturday, he would try mixing all manner of product with the colored gas, but with no success. Just as he was about to give up, he found a color neutralizer – the little yellow color pack that came with our white margarine did the trick. It turned the purple gas clear.

Slowly, but surely our roads began to improve, travel became less uncertain. By now our trails had become roads wide enough for two cars to pass and they were regularly graded and leveled. Each spring, as soon as the snows melted, the County imposed a Road Ban. No autos could travel the roads for several weeks until the surfaces had dried enough to prevent the wheels from making those deep ruts. Violating the Road Ban, except in cases of dire emergency, was punishable by fine.

A trip to Barrhead that I remember with sadness was the time Stanley, Mother and I started off for Grandfather Fridel's funeral in

April, 1944. Part way there, the car stalled. Stanley was an expert at repairs but this time he couldn't restart the engine, he couldn't figure out what was wrong. It was one of those rare times when I saw my mother cry.

"I won't even be on time for my own father's funeral."

Stanley got this helpless look on his face and I felt useless and of no help at all. It hurt to see Mother cry.

Eventually Stanley did restart the car, but we missed Grandfather's church service and arrived late at the graveside service.

Afterwards all of the distant family relatives gathered at Grandmother's house for a meal. As I watched all of my relatives that I had not seen for years, talking and visiting I thought,

"Why couldn't these people come to visit while Grandfather was alive? Why did it take a funeral to bring my relatives together?"

Tears were in my Aunt Annie's eyes as she tried to smile and serve food to the visiting family. I remember thinking, "If my father had just died, I don't think I could be that gracious."

Many horses were used to prepare the land for spring seeding.

This was a summer time job – hay making - 1937

Threshing time meant cutting the grain with a "binder".
This had to be done in the Fall of the year. My father was busy all year round.

Threshing Time

Fall was a busy time on the farm. Dad had to get his grain crop harvested. At first he used four horses to pull his binder, then a noisy Fordson tractor did the job of swathing the grain field as the binder tied the grain into bundles and dropped them along the field. Everyone helped at harvest time. Johnnie was six years old when he was driving the tractor while Dad operated the binder. At 5:30 Johnnie would quit and walk to the new homestead to bring home the cows for Mother and Helen to milk. The older boys gathered up the grain sheaves and stacked them into stooks, then we waited for the threshers to come. Only a very few better off farmers had threshing machines, they went from farm to farm in the order requested. Dad waited impatiently for his turn, praying for good weather and no rain.

When the threshing crew finally came, it was a happy time. The men were all hardworking, good natured local young lads who flirted with Valeria and me. Cooking for a crew was a full time job. Dad butchered a sheep, the meat barely lasted for the three days the crew threshed. Mrs. Hodges would come to help and she and Mother baked and cooked all day. The men had voracious appetites. No sooner was breakfast over than it was time to make the midmorning lunch of sandwiches and coffee to be carried out to the field. Dinner was served promptly at noon – lots of potatoes and gravy, no salads and few vegetables. The men were very critical of a farm wife's cooking and would discuss which lady made the best pies and cakes. After a big mid-day lunch it was time to start supper. The men continued working until it got too dark to see. When they finally came into the kitchen, each man stopped at the washstand, washed his face and hands, combed his hair and picked up the dipper that hung above the water pail and took a long drink. We all used that same dipper – it was the way it was done.

Dad would listen carefully to the 10:00 o'clock news for the latest price of grain. Our year's income depended on that price.

One fall when I was fourteen, a boyfriend of mine, Bill, was on the threshing crew. One afternoon after lunch I picked up a pitchfork and asked if I could help toss sheaves onto the hay rack. As we walked along behind the team of horses, stopping at each stook, throwing the sheaves, higher and higher onto the wagon, I felt strong and competent and full of energy, as if I could do this all day.

Then slowly and silently, all the sheaves I had piled up on my side of the hay rack slid onto the ground as I stared in surprise.

"Never mind," Bill said "I'll stack them all back for you and show you how to lay the sheaves so they stay in place."

Nothing is as simple as it looks, I thought.

That Long Lonesome Road

One by one, we older children left our little Poplar public school and went off to High School in Sangudo, first Stanley, then Vlad, then Helen. By the time I started High School, Stanley was already in University at Edmonton.

In the winter we three walked the 4½ miles to school but in the summers when the roads were dry we had bikes put together from various parts of salvaged older bikes. Our route was several miles of long hills, hard to pedal up, but a joy to coast downhill with the fresh wind in your face. If it rained the heavy gumbo mud plugged up our bicycle wheels and we either struggled pushing the bike along the grassy side of the road or stashing it in the bushes. One time, Stanley hid his bike and returned to find it stolen. Dad could not afford to buy him another.

During Alberta's short winter days it would still be dark when I left for school at 8:00 a.m. Vlad had chores to do so he usually left ten minutes after I did. When I reached the top of our hill, I would see ahead of me a solid, unbroken sheet of snow, a 1½ mile slash of white ribbon between the dense woods on either side. I had to "break trail." An occasional rabbit track across my path would be a comforting sight on this lonely stretch. It was very reassuring to know my brother was behind me.

Then he too left for University and I was trail-blazing alone, no other kids along that dark road for 3½ miles. Half a mile from our house, an old abandoned barn stood on the old Sager place. An up-stairs door on the hay loft squeaked eerily back and forth in the wind and a resident owl hooted its lonely call sending a sense of fear into the heart of this not-so-brave 15 year old hurrying past in the dark. Common sense told me there was no cause for alarm but I was always very relieved when I had passed Sager's barn. Years later, when I told Mother about my unease she said,

"Why didn't you tell me? Your Dad would have done something

about it."

One summer while Vlad was still in High School, Dad said Vlad and I could drive to school in the Model A. We were delighted and felt very important giving rides ot the "Dorm Kids" who lived in the school dormitory 2 miles out of town. Then Dad said he didn't want us driving so far out of our way and we were told, "No more rides to Dorm Kids and come straight home."

One lad from the dorm asked for a ride. Vlad said "No!" The boy took the Model A crank and said, "You don't get this back until you promise to drive me to the dorm." Our car could only be started with a crank so we were held hostage, knowing we couldn't go counter to our Dad's orders.

The boy stood in front of our local grocery store, holding the crank under his arm.

I said to Vlad, "I'm going to get that crank from him."

I crept up quietly and carefully behind the boy, grabbed the crank, and with all the force I could muster, swung it backwards away from him.

Crash! Crash! The crank hit the plate glass store front window scattering glass in all directions. For a few moments, the lad and I stood stunned unable to believe what had happened.

"Jesus!" he blurted out and bolted away, one fast disappearing young man.

I stood there frightened and wondering what to do. With a great deal of anxiety, I forced myself to walk into the store and approached the owner behind the counter.

"I broke your window," I said in a quivering voice.

"Yes, Helen. You can see I am waiting on a customer. You will have to wait your turn, so please step away until I'm finished."

Those next few minutes as I stood waiting for the owner to talk with me were some of the longest minutes of my life.

When Dad heard about the incident, he went immediately to the Sangudo High School Board. The next day a decree was issued and posted.

"NO MORE RIDES TO BE GIVEN BY
THE LISS FAMILY TO ANY DORMITORY
BOYS OR GIRLS."

My parents told me they never received a bill for the plate glass window replacement. Mother thought they had billed the boy who ran away and praised me for having the courage to stay and face the store owner.

In the years that I walked to High School alone, there were two scary incidents that frightened me.

One winter morning, from the top of our hill, I could see a mile ahead of me, a dark figure walking in my direction through the deep snow. We know everyone in our district but as the figure came nearer, I could not recognize any of our neighbors. Close and closer came this stranger, walking with his head down, never waving, never acknowledging that he saw me. As he passed alongside me, he never spoke or looked up. I felt very uneasy. If I screamed, no one would hear me, if I tried to run, where would I run to? I was afraid to look back, but when I finally did, the figure was still plodding along, head down, just as he had before.

My second scare happened one summer afternoon while walking home from school. A car stopped alongside me and the male driver offered me a ride. Rides were always welcome so I got in. When I asked him how far he was going, he replied, "Mayerthorpe," but when we got to the corner where he should have turned and dropped me off, he continued north towards our farm. I didn't like the way he looked at me. When we reached the turn-off to our farm, he turned off the engine, reaching out his arms to me.

"Come here!"

With lightning fast reflex I opened the car door, jumped out and started running the ¼ mile to our house. Thank God the wire gate was open.

Mother said when I came into the kitchen my face was white and she knew I had been frightened. I never saw that man again, and we never learned who he was.

My father told me many times that if a man ever accosted me, I was to try to poke my finger into his eye or hit him in the groin. Later Vlad said, "What Dad means is punch him in the balls." That well-rehearsed advise saved me one evening while walking the two blocks from the Community Hall into the village.

Vlad and I had been to a movie at the hall. Our movies always began with the audience standing to sing, "Oh Canada" and ended with us singing "God Save the King." My brother and I decided at the earliest moment after our patriotic song, I would dash out, hurry "uptown" and commandeer a booth in our only café. He would follow as soon as he could start the car.

As I hurried along, suddenly out of nowhere, I was grabbed from behind, one arm encircled my neck, the other reaching under my skirt. I could feel hot, panting breath on my neck. I knew exactly what to do – I struggled, hit the boy where Dad and Vlad had instructed me and I ran.

When I arrived home, I told my parents what had happened and that my attacker was a neighbor boy.

"I'll kill that son-of-a-bitch," my father exploded.

A few days later an R.C.M.P. drove into our yard and asked to speak to me.

"Tell me exactly what happened, Helen."

Mother stood beside me as I recounted my unpleasant experience, "And then he put his hand down where he shouldn't have." As I spoke, the Mountie wrote it all down and when he finished, he read it to me.

"Is this how you remember it, Helen?"

"Yes," I replied.

"Then please sign your full name here at the bottom."

"I'll take care of this matter and your neighbor will never bother you again."

The spring that I was in Grade XII, heavy rains fell, the break-up of the ice and accumulated debris washed out the bridge over the Pembina River. The Alberta Highways Department decided to re-route the road. A new bridge and new access road to Sangudo, added an extra mile to my trek to High School, making a 5½ mile journey each morning and afternoon. It became too tiring for me and Mother arranged for me to board at the Hepburn's home in the village. Their only pay was an occasional quart of cream or a roasting chicken. They were very good to me and I was forever grateful to them.

Dominion Illustration Station

When John first came to his homestead, he heard some neighbors say,

"That John Liss is a fool! We are working every day chopping down trees and what is he doing? He is planting trees. What a foolhardy way to spend precious time."

John was indeed planting trees. He investigated where he could obtain seedlings from the government and planted shelter belts all around his farm buildings. Manitoba maples, ash, elm and spruce protected his farmstead from winter's cold and drifting snows and offered shelter to his animals.

In all his horticultural efforts, our dad had been supported and aided by his father, Grandfather Pozarzyski. It was Grandfather who left Alberta a botanical legacy. Working in the woods one day, south of his homestead, he discovered a native cherry that he recognized as an unusual fruit. Grandfather dug up the bush and Dad planted it along the side of our house. When Dad contacted the University of Alberta, research determined that Grandfather's cherry was indeed an unnamed variety. It was then given an official botanical name, "The Mary Liss Pin Cherry." Over the years it has been carefully propagated and nurtured and today the Mary Liss Pin Cherry grows across Canada, a lasting tribute to our mother.

Our dad set aside a tract of land for an orchard and began experimenting with grafting and cross-pollination of fruit trees. I remember carefully weeding his small apple seedlings with a tablespoon. I would never have envisioned that thirty years later he would have more apples and crabapples than he could give away.

In 1937, our farm was selected by the Dominion of Canada as an Illustration Station where experimental work was carried out under government supervision. Testing of new grain varieties, new ways of fertilizing and ways to improve farming were all designed to help the immigrant homesteaders. Our family was very proud when a huge

Indigo Bunting

Special thoughts from
Ms. Helen Smart

Aug. 10, 2007

Thank you, Chuck
for wanting a copy
of my book. I hope
you and Shirley enjoy
it.

The price is $20.00

Thanks, Helen.

Helen Smart
7842 Day Dr.
Goleta, CA 93117-1099

metal sign supported by two sturdy poplar poles was erected on our farm facing the rural road.

Illustration Station
John Liss – Operator
co-operating with
Dominion Experimental Farms

Dominion Illustration Station Sign – John Liss 1937

From then on, we had to keep careful records of all our farm activities, what we fed the animals, the weights of their newborn, the amount of eggs collected daily. My job was to weigh each cow's milk production. I hooked the milk pail over a hanging spring scale and carefully recorded it daily. I felt important to be part of a Canadian operation.

The high point of the year was Field Day. The government posted huge signs in conspicuous places, 18 inches by 24 inches, advertising the coming event. In 4 inch high letters across the top of the poster, big, bold, block print said,

FIELD DAY

Listed below were all the topics to be discussed, all pertinent to farm life and all delivered by agricultural experts. One year the topics were –

Winter Egg Production
Forage Crops
Control of Field and Garden Insects
Control of Soil Drifting – Lantern slide show

To us children, a lantern slide show was as good as a movie. The day of the Field Day was a festive friendly event. A huge tent was set up in our back yard with benches arranged under its shade. In one corner of our yard near the well house Dad had a smoke house, a small 4' x 4' building with a big door. Stanley and Vlad posted a sign on the door.

"This is not what you think
it is. Follow the arrows to
the outhouse north of the house
beyond the willows."

Farmers and their families came from surrounding communities from miles away, anxious to listen, learn and ask questions. The men wore their best (and only) suits and the women came in neat house-dresses. After the lectures and lantern slides, everyone traipsed into the field to examine the experimental plots and discuss the merits of various methods of fertilizing.

Then came the fun part we children liked best. Mother made a huge copper boiler full of coffee, everyone brought their lunches and neighbors visited until it was time to leave to do farm chores. Mother looked so happy chatting with neighbors she seldom saw. As kids we never realized how lonely Mother was for women to talk with. We kids drank Mother's coffee and no one said, "You know you aren't supposed to drink coffee. It will stunt your growth."

Field Day ended on a happy note. It had not rained and the farmers left with new ideas and valuable information.

Alas! World War II started. John Liss joined the Canadian Army and the Dominion Illustration Station was forced to close after only five years of operation.

We were all sorry to see the end of this worthy undertaking.

Arthur Vlad Liss

When I was growing up, I felt very proud of my two older brothers. Stan was worldly, he knew words I had never heard of, he could fix anything that broke, he could start the old Model A when no one else could. He was invincible.

Vlad was tall, slender and strong with a head of thick curly blonde hair – I called him my Greek God. His infectious laugh made us laugh and we never could count his list of lady friends. He was inventive, always trying out new ideas.

There was a daily after-school routine in our family. We came home, drank the hot soup Mother had for us, changed from school clothes into the work clothes that hung on the back porch, then set off to do the farm chores. The boys each took their coal oil lantern, engulfed by a pool of yellow light as they walked about. Vlad was always late for supper, always the last one in and Mother became concerned.

"That boy has too much work to do," she told Father. "He's always the last one in and we have to relieve him of some of his duties."

When Father investigated, he found that Vlad had a book in the hay loft, a book in the granary and a book in the sheep shed. As he went about his chores, he would stop in each building and read a chapter by lantern light. No wonder he was the last in.

Vlad had ingenious solutions to all problems. Mother and I usually did the milking, but one time we both had to leave. Mother told Vlad to see that the cows were milked.

"Are the cows milked?" she asked him when we returned.

An odd look came over my brother's face. "Y-yes" he replied hesitantly. Mother discovered later that the cows had indeed been milked but not as she and I would have done the job. Vlad had accomplished the task effortlessly by turning the cows into the pen where their eager calves waited, suckling their mothers dry.

Vlad had an efficient way of drying the dishes. One Saturday when we left him to take care of that job, we returned to see him hastily emptying the warming oven above the stove where he had placed everything to dry.

On Saturdays my job was to bake enough cookies for our school lunches for the week. I carefully counted out how many would be needed, then Vlad would come in, grab a handful and exclaim "Boy! Are you ever a good cook." No matter where I hid the cookies, he would find them.

Stanley came to my rescue. He said "I'll hide those cookies where Vlad will never find them." And he did. He hid the pan of cookies in the unlit fire box of the little living room stove. Vlad never found them and I had enough cookies for next week's lunches.

One Saturday when our parents were away for the afternoon, Vlad decided to make some beer. He mixed up a brew, poured it into empty beer bottles he had found along the road, corked the bottles, then carried them upstairs and stashed them beneath his dresser. My friend Lucy was visiting and Vlad swore us both to secrecy.

"Don't you dare tell anyone about this beer," he admonished.

When our parents drove into the yard, Mother was not even out of the car when Lucy ran up.

"Mrs. Liss! Mrs. Liss! Vlad is making beer."

Nothing was done about Vlad's beer but days later as we were seated at supper we heard "Pop! Pop! Pop" as the beer corks exploded against the bottom of Vlad's dresser.

"Let's all have a taste of your efforts," Dad said with a smile.

As we grew into our teens, Vlad and I developed a close friendship. We enjoyed each other's company, we laughed a lot and I always felt comfortable, protected and safe whenever I was with my brother.

Sometimes, though, I thought he was too protective. Driving to Sangudo one Saturday in the old Model A, we passed a road grader operated by a boy I liked.

"Oh! Stop Vlad! Stop! I want to talk to Norm."

Vlad kept on driving and made no effort to stop. Instead he said with firmness,

"Ladies don't stop in the middle of the road to talk to boys. If he wants to see you, he knows where you live."

Another time my brother's firmness and protective care of me ended a good time I was having. Vlad and I were with a large group of young people enjoying a Sunday picnic on the river bank when my brother came up to me and announced, "Come on, Helen. We're going home."

"Why? I'm having such a good time."

"You are going home. There is alcohol being served here and I don't want you associating with people who are drinking. Come on."

And that was that. We left.

One sunny fall day, Vlad, my High School friend Sylvia and I eagerly set off to go blueberry picking in the sandhills 30 miles west of us. We were fortunate in finding a splendid berry patch and happily began picking the plump berries. Birds were all around us in the jackpines and we thrilled at the sight of a beautiful little red fox that ran across the trail only a few feet from us.

Then suddenly the sun disappeared and a drenching shower caught us all by surprise. Within a few minutes the sun returned but by now we were soaked, wet and dripping. Vlad took one look at Sylvia and me, water from our hair running down our face, our sodden clothing hugging our bodies.

"You girls can't keep those damp clothes on or you will catch cold. I'm going to dry them for you."

He made a small fire, got two old blankets from the car, fastened the bigger one to two jackpines to make a privacy screen and handed the other blanket to Sylvia and me.

"If you two girls get behind this screen and hand me your pants and shirts I'll try to dry them for you as fast as possible."

While Sylvia and I huddled together under the old blanket, Vlad draped our pants and shirts over long sticks and patiently held them over the fire until our garments dried. As he handed our clothing to us across the top of our privacy screen, he smiled.

"Now you don't have to spend the rest of the day in uncomfortable damp clothing and I don't have to worry about you girls getting double pneumonia."

It felt good to be dry.

One summer Vlad was working at a horticultural station in Manyberries, in southern Alberta to save enough money to be able to go back to University. He was visiting the farm in August when he said,

"Helen, if you will go back to Manyberries with me I'll give you a radio and pay your train fare."

I was excited and delighted when I asked Mother if I could go.

"Let's go talk to your Father."

The three of us, Mother, Vlad and Helen walked north of the house to where Dad was repairing a snake fence. When he heard about Vlad's offer, he sighed.

"Oh, Helen. You know how much work there is for Mother in the summer. She needs you to help with the garden and the canning. Mother has so much to do."

"Let her go, John. She's never been to Southern Alberta and I can manage without her for two weeks."

The long train ride with several transfers, the miles and miles of flat prairie, meals in the dining car with white tablecloths and white-jacketed waiters – everything was an adventure. When we arrived in Manyberries I was lodged in the Supervisor's house while the family was away – a big modern house all to myself.

The countryside all around us was barren, brown almost treeless prairie, but Manyberries horticultural farm was a green heaven of shelterbelts, hedges, green lawns, gardens and neatly tended homes. Vlad introduced me to the McCutions, a family he called 'The Big Gear and the Little Clutches', to Merle and Blondie who made the best coffee I ever tasted and to the McQueen Family who made me feel very welcome.

The Smuggler's apparatus – from a distance.

The day after I arrived, Vlad said, "Come on. Let's go see the country." He took me in his "car", a metal shell with no seats, no doors, a skeleton of what once was. His seat was a box, mine was a sack of oats draped over the frame. We bounded off, the ground rolling by under me, nothing to cling to but my brother; it was scary fun as I watched the flat prairie beneath my feet. I could almost reach down and touch the grass.

That Sunday, Vlad announced,
"I'm taking you to the United States for a visit."

This is a close-up view of the Smuggler's Apparatus.

Little did I know that a smuggling expedition was ahead of me. We drove west across the Milk River, then south to Coutts and on in the general direction of Sweetgrass, Montana. A short distance from the U.S.-Canadian border, we left the main road and followed a trail through the treeless badlands, stopping where a river separated the two countries. Three young men were awaiting us, waving a welcome to us and greeting Vlad by name. I could see a sturdy wooden "A" frame structure about 30 feet high on the Alberta side and a similar

"A" frame structure on the Montana side. A series of metal cables and pulleys connected the two "A" frames and a box-like one-man gondola hung from the cables that spanned the river. There were no houses or people around. One of Vlad's friends climbed the "A" frame tower and got into the gondola.

"Okay everyone. Stand guard while I cross over to the U.S. to buy a supply of cigarettes."

Hand over hand, he ferried himself over to the Montana side. One after another, Vlad, his two other friends and I ferried ourselves in the sturdy little gondola over to the U.S. side where a car waited. One of Vlad's buddies drove us all to Sweetgrass, Montana where we all bought less costly U.S. cigarettes. Since neither Vlad nor I smoked our loot was given to the three young men. We "gondolad" ourselves back to the Canadian side, Vlad and I hopped into his funny little car and had an uneventful drive back to Manyberries.

I left Manyberries that morning as a law-abiding citizen and now I was returning as a law-breaking smuggler.

Hobart Peters, one of the men who worked on the station asked if I would like a ride in his little private plane. As we flew over the coulees and farmsteads I thought, "Whatever else I do in life, nothing can thrill me as much as this, my first ride in an airplane."

One evening Hobart came to visit me at the Supervisor's house. He sat down in a small wooden rocking chair, gently rocking back and forth, when suddenly the delicate chair collapsed. Hobart's long legs went in all directions as the startled man lay amid the broken pieces.

I laughed! Hobart never came to visit me again but I often wondered what the Supervisor thought when he came home and found his little chair all busted.

It was hot in Manyberries, around 90° each day. A huge water tank with a big 'NO SWIMMING IN TANK' sign across the front was on the station property. Vlad and I climbed up the 25 foot long metal ladder and jumped in for a refreshing swim. No one saw us or reported us so we took a dip each day. When I think of the stupidity of two young people swimming in a deep water tank away from people I shudder at what could have happened. Our guardian angel was indeed watching over us.

The two weeks slipped by and all too soon I was on the train heading back to Sangudo with my radio and a head full of memories.

I would never have imagined that this visit with my beloved brother Vlad would be our last.

John Liss – Calgary, Alberta - 1941

The War Comes to Our Town

Our lives were about to drastically change. A sense of unease was developing in our community. Something was happening in Europe that didn't sound good. Germany, in "The Old Country" as our immigrant neighbors called it, was showing signs of aggression under someone called Hitler. Our parents had long, serious discussions with visiting neighbors; worried looks and talk of another war dominated the gatherings. One Sunday in September, 1939, the radio was on all day long. Our family was quiet and subdued. In the late afternoon came the inevitable and dreaded news. Britain had declared war on Germany!

To this day I can hear my father's long, deep, sad, sigh. "God help us all."

Everyone got behind the war effort. The young neighbor boys all joined up and those farm lads looked so mature and handsome in their Army uniforms. We children bought 25 cent war savings stamps and saved aluminum foil. We wrote regularly to the boys overseas. No one complained about rationing, but since we never bought much it hardly affected us.

I would see my parents talking together quietly but I could never hear any part of their conversations. They looked so serious! Then one day in 1941 came the announcement that our dad was going to join the Canadian Army. Dad had long conversations with Stanley and Vlad. They would have to help Mother run the farm. "How," I worried, "Could we ever manage without our Dad?"

The inevitable day arrived. Today Father was leaving us. He was going off to war. Far to the west we could hear the hooting of the approaching train as we hugged and kissed him goodbye, Mother standing quietly beside him, fighting back her tears. As the train pulled slowly away from the station platform, Mother thought "Now that John can't see me, I think I shall really cry," but at that moment one of our neighbors, Mr. Chisma, approached and asked if he could have a ride home, and naturally, she could not break down and cry in front of a neighbor.

"I'll have a good cry when I get home," she told herself – but as the car drove into the yard, my oldest brother, Stanley rushed up.

"Grab a hay fork!" he yelled. "There are dark clouds approaching from the west. We've got to cock that hay I cut yesterday in the north meadow or it will be ruined if it rains."

"I guess I'll postpone my cry until this evening," Mother promised herself as she rushed to put on her work clothes. All day long Mother and my brothers worked furiously cocking and piling the hay to keep it from getting wet. By nightfall when the downpour came, the hay was safely stacked. By evening, Mother was too exhausted to cry as she flung herself gratefully into bed. The next morning it seemed ridiculous to cry over something so long since past. Over the years Mother was able to truthfully say that when her husband went off to the war, she had not shed a single tear.

Mother and Helen
Shear Sheep

One of the summers while Dad was away in the Army and my brothers were busy with the harvest, Mother decided that she and I should shear our sheep. I was confident that I knew how it should be done. Several years earlier I had watched a professional sheep shearer effortless snipping away at the thick mass, leaving an intact fleece that fell like a fluffy blanket at his feet, as the neatly shorn animal bounded off.

Something went wrong at the start for Mother and me. Our bewildered ewe refused to cooperate and remain still. To keep the nervous animal quiet, we tied its front feet together, then bound together its hind feet. The terrified animal tried to hobble away in short, powerful leaps.

Mother grasped the ewe to restrain her while I attempted to clip. As my unsteady hands made jabs at the sheep's pelt, the wool dropped in miserable little clumps. Each time the frightened animal jerked, my sharp clippers nicked its skin; soon the poor creature was spotted with evidence of my ineptitude.

When we finally untied the ropes from its legs, our shorn sheep lay quivering in an apparent state of shock, then giving a pathetic bleat, rushed off to the comfort of the flock, a most irregularly, unevenly and inexpertly sheared animal.

Mother and I sheared two more sheep that day and towards the end our technique had improved, but not much!

For as far back as I can remember we always had a flock of sheep. In the fall after the sheep were shorn, we washed the wool and mailed it off to a factory to be made into blankets, yardage and skeins of wool. When we got the finished products back, we always knew it was our own wool because we would see bits of our own farm's weeds and burrs in the material. The blankets lasted for sixty years, becoming softer and thinner as they were laundered over the years. When my brother, Stanley attended his first year at the University of Alberta, his only pair of trousers was one made from our course, heavy wool.

We all learned to knit and made mitts and socks from the thick yarn, but the day our father returned from an auction sale with a knitting machine was a real blessing. I watched my oldest brother as he threaded the wool into the machine, then whirled the handle around and around. To my amazement a long tube of sock emerged. Then he made the heel, forward and reverse, forward and reverse. "How does he do that?" I asked with the awe of a twelve year old sister who thought her brother could do anything.

Life was not easy for our mother when she was left to run the farm. Besides all the daily chores, the crops had to be planted in the spring and harvested in the fall. Hay had to be mowed and stacked and hauled to the barn for winter's animal feed. When animals had their young in the spring, she often had to assist. When a mother sow had a large litter, there would often be a small, rejected animal, the "runt". Mother put that piglet into a box and carried it to a warm spot under the kitchen stove where we fed it from a milk bottle. Each animal represented material wealth and had to be saved.

One cold fall day, a faithful old black horse, Buck, lay in the barnyard unable to stand. As he struggled, he became weaker and weaker and it became apparent that Buck was dying. A strong, cold wind blew in from the west. Mother took her pitchfork and stacked forkloads of hay around the dying animal to shield him from the biting wind.

"This is my compassionate mother," I thought. "Buck is going to die but Mother is trying to make him as comfortable as she can in his last hours."

Why didn't she call the veterinarian? We never had a vet in Sangudo until after World War II when a displaced person from Europe came to Sangudo. When animals got sick, there was no one to help the farmers.

Mother had depended on Stanley all her life and now more than ever she needed his backing. One evening as we all sat in the living room reading or doing homework, Mother asked my younger brother, Ted,

"Have you fed the chickens?"

"No."

"Don't you think you better do so?"

Several minutes went by and Ted did not get up from his chair.

Stanley looked up from his homework.

He looked directly at Ted and in a firm, strong, authoritative voice said,

"Did you hear your mother? <u>MOVE!</u>"

None of us ever argued or dared disobey our brother Stanley.

Mother had undertaken a demanding job. Four hundred and eighty acres to oversee and no husband. Her two oldest sons were a great help to her but when Stanley went to University that left only Mother and Vlad. The younger boys had their daily chores but I wasn't much help. By then I was walking 4½ miles to the High School in the village and I was exhausted when I came home.

I missed my father terribly. There was a big emptiness in our family during the years he was away and I wished the war would end so he could come home.

In 1943, our dad received a medical discharge from the Army and returned to the farm, a sick man. Painful ulcers and arthritis plagued him. Small things irritated him and it was many years before he became well and the father I remembered.

We knew he was back to his former self, ready for any challenges, when he announced his latest plan to Mother.

"Mary, I have always remembered that lovely land in the Peace River County that I had to forfeit in 1912. It was such a rich and fertile soil – I could do wonders with that land. I would like us to go back to the Peace River area and look for a homestead."

Mother looked at him in surprise. For a few seconds she did not speak.

"John! I homesteaded with my father. I homesteaded with you. I am NOT homesteading again."

Dad did not argue or pursue the subject. Mother did not often take a stand, but when she did, the firm tone of her voice meant there was no need for further discussion.

A sad little memory from my very early childhood came back to me. Dad had said to Mother,

"You never sing any more, Mary."

"There's nothing to sing about" had been her reply.

Mother had paid her homesteading dues – she didn't need to do so again.

Speaking with Mother years later about her time on the farm without a husband, I asked,

"You had so much responsibility on your shoulders, raising us kids, running the farm, tending the animals, mending fences, repairing things that broke, weren't those lonely, hard years for you?"

"Oh, there was a lot of good that resulted. I learned to be independent and sure of myself. I could walk into the bank and ask for a loan like any farmer. It was a positive experience for a shy person like me."

Our mother was a remarkable lady who could always find some redeeming aspect in every situation.

It always bothered me that it took a war for our family to have a steady stream of cash. While our dad was in the Army, a monthly check came to Mother enabling her to finally buy things from the Eaton's catalogue that we needed; shoes, underwear, jackets and even the luxury of Mother's first pair of nylon stockings.

From Heartbreak to
Better Times

A devastating and heartbreaking event shattered our family in the summer of 1946. Stanley, an engineering student at the University of Saskatchewan, was working during the summer for the Hudson's Bay Mining and Smelting Company in Flin Flon, Manitoba. He was diving in a northern lake when he fractured three vertebrae in his neck, leaving him completely paralyzed from his neck down.

Mother immediately left for Edmonton, staying with Auntie Oly until she could make arrangements for the long train trip across the prairie to Flin Flon. She remained with her oldest son most of the summer. Mother knew Stanley's determination would overcome his paralysis when she watched him one afternoon as she sat by his hospital bed. She saw his finger twitch, then slowly, slowly his hand moved upwards across his chest, until one hour later, his hand reached his chin.

In an exasperated voice, her son asked, "Mother will you please scratch my nose? I've been trying for an hour." It broke our hearts to hear her tell us of our strong 6 foot brother lying motionless in a cast, two hooks under his cheek bones, holding his head immobile and upright to relieve pressure on his neck. As soon as fall work was over, Dad left to spend the winter near his son, working as a carpenter to support himself.

Stan endured a long hospital stay, months of therapy and learned to walk again. On his first trip to the farm after his accident, I remember our Mother standing at the sink, looking across the yard as Stanley navigated slowly and awkwardly toward the house, dragging each leg in a painful uncoordinated effort. Tears slid down her face as she watched her oldest child, the boy who had been so capable and able now restricted in his movements.

In 1948, Stanley married Dorothy Young, a talented lady he met during his hospital stay. With her loyal support, he was able to live a rewarding and productive life.

We Lisses enjoy telling people that Dorothy is writer Scott Young's sister and singer Neil Young's aunt.

Again pain and devastating heartbreak struck the Liss family in June, 1949. Vlad had been working for the Parks Department in Flin Flon, Manitoba. I was being married in Sangudo on June 17, 1949 and Vlad was to be part of the wedding party. He flew into Edmonton late one evening, decided not to wait for next day's 5:00 p.m. Greyhound bus to Sangudo and hired a taxi to drive him the 80 miles to the farm that evening.

"Sure the taxi cost a lot but it was worth it to see everyone a day earlier," he smiled.

The wedding reception took place on the front lawn of our parent's house. Mother's colorful garden was in full bloom, my younger brothers had mowed the lawns, trimmed the caragana hedges and weeded the gardens. Everything looked tidy and neat.

Without anyone's knowledge, Vlad, ever the rascal, had poured a fifth of vodka into the punch and snickered when the guests said,

"This sure is good punch. May I have a refill?"

After the wedding, Vlad flew back to Flin Flon. Three days later, on June 20, 1949, he was dead.

He had gone fishing with a friend when the friend's clothing caught fire from a cigarette. The friend jumped into the water to put out the fire, but he couldn't swim and Vlad could see the man was in trouble. Vlad dove into the cold lake, pushed his buddy into the boat, then disappeared from sight, probably from cramps due to the frigid water.

The sorrow over the sudden death of our brother, Arthur Vlad at 24 years of age remains with us forever.

Life in our community changed for the better after World War II. In 1947 oil was discovered in Northern Alberta. At last the province had money to build and repair rural roads. In 1950, through the efforts of John Liss, all the farmers organized to supply power poles and rural electrification finally came to the neighborhood. Now everything was easier; drudgery was replaced by an electric switch; the change in a farmer's life was incredible. Every farmer could tell you the exact day when they "got the power."

During the years that John Liss had farmed on the Paddle River Flats, he and the farm families in the river's flood plain were at the mercy of unpredictable spring floods on The Flats. The gentle Paddle River so tranquil in the summer, as a result of rains and snow melt from the foothills, flooded, inundating thousands of acres of land from Rochfort Bridge to Barrhead. These severe floods plagued the valley farmers for decades, isolating their homes, eroding the fine soil, damaging their buildings and fences and drowning cows and sheep. An aerial survey in 1975 reported roads under 4 feet of water, floating machinery and debris, dead animals and cattle marooned on small areas of higher ground.

Enough is enough!

John Liss and the affected farmers realized that only a strong united voice could move the government to action. They organized and began to fight. John and Mary Liss, their sons Edward and Ted and a group of dedicated neighbors actively lobbied to keep the Paddle Valley Flood Control issue before the government and the public. At last the government began a serious search for solutions. In 1980 construction was started on a dam to control the Paddle River waters and relieve the farmers of the uncertainty of those disastrous floods they had endured for so many years.

A sixty year dream of John Liss had finally come to be.

The Spring floods covering the roadway.

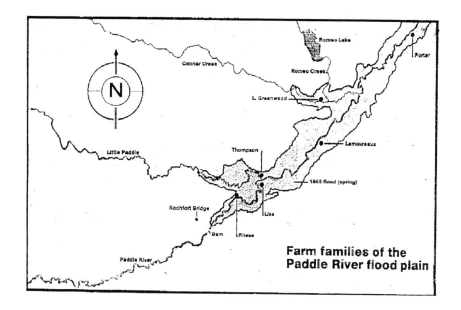

Farm families of the Paddle River flood plain

John liked to fish but he did not feel it was right for an elderly fisherman to pay for the sport. He was instrumental in having fishing licenses eliminated for Seniors in Alberta.

He ran for political office several times and while he never won an election, he never lost a political argument.

The Indians of the Alexis Reserve needed a farm advisor, so John volunteered. All went well for many years and a mutual respect developed between the Alexis Peoples and our dad. But when a series of dry summers came and no rain fell for their crops, they blamed him. After all wasn't John in charge of their agricultural needs? Couldn't he control the rain?

"I don't want them to think I was their God," John said when he decided to resign.

Our parents gave thanks daily for the wonders of electric power and natural gas. Dad no longer had to pump water for an hour – he flipped a switch. But it was Mother whose life was amazingly easier, indoor plumbing, hot water, an electric washing machine, a deep freeze, a refrigerator, automatic heat – no more frigid mornings, no kerosene lamps to light every night.

"If only we had had natural gas and electric power when all you kids were little," Mother often said.

John Liss turned over farm operations to Ted, his son who shared his farming interest. Now our parents had the luxury of time — time to pursue their horticultural interests, time to engage in community work. No more cows to milk, no more chickens to feed, no more sheep to shear. Their fruit orchards became a showplace, cherries, plums, pears and more apples and crabapples than they could give away. Every fall people came to the Liss Farm to gather seeds and seedlings. It pleased our parents to know that the Mary Liss Cherry grew across Canada – from Ontario to British Columbia. Life was good!

A new car and good roads made for pleasant drives as our Dad campaigned for his political party. After one such trip, Mother and Dad had reservations at the McDonald Hotel in Edmonton, a first-time treat at this prestigious hotel. Mother looked forward to a hot bath in a big tub, but when she went to start the water, neither she nor Dad could figure out how to turn on "that new-fangled faucet," so Mother did her usual basin bath and laughed when she told us the story.

"Why didn't you phone and ask the hotel for help?" I asked.

"Oh, well, we had already undressed and we didn't want to bother them," was her reply.

A Final Tribute

The Liss Farm

John and Mary Liss had become successful farmers and respected citizens. When asked what contributed to his success John replied, "A good wife, a co-operative family and helpful government agriculturists."

The parents took pride in their children's successful careers.

Kenneth became the liquor distributor for Western Canada. Stanley, an electrical engineer became part of management at the Hudson's Bay Mining and Smelting Company in Flin Flon, Manitoba. Vlad's untimely death ended a promising career in horticulture. Helen became a teacher and a real estate agent. Edward retired after 25 years in the Canadian Air Force. Ted took over the family farm. Valeria spent six years in the Air Force as a Lieutenant, then earned a degree and began teaching. She was awarded the Queen's Golden Jubilee Medal for her civic work. John, the youngest, retired from the Army with the rank of Major.

In tribute to the horticultural efforts of John and Mary Liss, the Dominion of Canada erected an historic cairn on the Liss farm, a fitting memorial to two pioneers who helped build Alberta and Canada.

ALBERTA HISTORIC MARKER
LISS FARM
Sec. 24, T57, R.7, W5M
Site of the first
Paddle River Valley
Dominion Farm Illustration Station
Operated 1938-1943 under
Supervision of
Lacombe Experimental Farm
in Cooperation with
John Liss and family

Their ashes rest nearby on the land they loved.

John Pozarzyski Liss
1892-1986
Last of the old time immigrant pioneers.
With his hands, backbone and integrity,
he helped build Alberta and Canada.
His soul and monument are his land.

Mary Martha Fridel Liss
1903-1990
Pioneer wife and mother.
At her husband's side for 64 years on this virgin homestead.
She raised 7 grateful children with neither running water,
plumbing, electricity nor complaints.
Self-denying. Understanding. Composed.

The historic Cairn and John and Mary Liss Memorial

Obituary

Mary Fridel Liss
1903 – 1990
Pioneer Wife and Mother

At her husband's side for 64 years on the Liss Farm homestead. She raised 7 self-reliant children with neither running water, gas, plumbing, electricity – nor complaints. Wholesome, self-denying, composed.

A chapter of Alberta's history ended with the passing of Mary Liss, a true pioneer wife and mother. Those who had the pleasure of knowing her will never forget her inspiring cheerful disposition and innumerable kindnesses to everyone with whom she came in contact. Nothing daunted her: neither the hard toil and isolation of a virgin homestead, the glacial Alberta winters in a log cabin, the destruction of her home by fire, the deprivation of the Great Depression, the loneliness of World War II when her husband John was away in the armed service, her oldest son Stanley's paralyzing accident, nor the drowning death of her second son Vlad at age 24. Self-pity was not her hallmark.

She delighted in each spring, and in each new grandchild and great-grandchild. She applauded each individual's successes and sympathized with their problems. All of her children remember their childhood's fondly, and all in turn sent their children back to the ancestral farm to stay awhile with their grandparents so as to benefit from the wholesome environment close to the soil. Mary and John always welcomed each grandchild as an individual personality to be reared and cherished. John Liss, a real patriarch of the family, provided an excellent role model of what devoted hard work, backbone, integrity, and community spirit could do. But it was the motherly Mary, whose kindness, understanding, and unflappable good-sense were lovingly appreciated by all of her brood. She was patient, understanding, composed.

How did this inspiring woman get to Sangudo? She was born Mary Martha Fridel on 29 March 1903 in the village of Nowosieliza, Snyatyn District in the formerly Polish province of Galicia of the Austrian-Hungarian Empire. Her father was a coal miner, and when Mary was three years old, her family and several uncles emigrated to Alberta, Canada to work as coal miners near Edmonton. Her father's health broke down in the mines, so he moved to a homestead near Barrhead in May 1911. All of the family's possessions were in a wagon pulled by oxen during the 3-day trip from Edmonton to the log shack on the new homestead. All of the family worked on the homestead during the summers, and the father went back to work in the coal mines during the winters to get money to pay for their next year's bills. Mary and her brothers walked the 3 miles to the Paddle River school where she completed grade 8. Then, at the age of 16, she went to stay with relatives in Edmonton to continue her schooling through grade 10. She earned her keep there by helping with the housework.

Mary met her future husband John Liss in late fall 1921, when she was 18 years old. Three months later on February 24, 1922, they were married by the RC priest in her parents' log house. The delightful story of their courtship is a reminder of how things have changed since "the good old days". John Liss was 29 years old and had been widowed almost two years. He was homesteading near Sangudo and concluded that he needed a wife to survive there. After making inquiries re local eligible girls, and hearing about Mary, he hitched up his team and drove the 35 miles from Sangudo to Barrhead (a long-day's drive cross country through 35 barbed wire gates) looking for her parents' farm. On his first visit, John met the family – including Mary – stayed overnight, and returned home. (Mary said: "I knew what he had come for, and knew that he would be back" – even though they had not talked alone.) A month later John returned, and asked Mr. Fridel for Mary's hand. When her father asked whether such was acceptable to her, Mary replied "Yes." The family then made plans for the wedding and John again went home. A month later he returned and they were married. The day after the wedding Mary sewed many things that she needed on her mother's sewing machine. It would be 5 more years before she had her own sewing machine which they bought from a neighbor for $10.

Finding Mary was like winning the lottery. If John had looked the world over with the assistance of a modern computer-dating service, he could not have found a better mate. Mary even learned to speak

John's Polish dialect after they were married. The new couple drove in the sleigh back to John's Sangudo homestead where they lived until John's death 64 years later in 1986. The Lisses had 7 children – 5 boys and 2 girls. The kids were all provided with the first year at University – but then were expected to make it on their own. All of the children are successful, self-reliant citizens, with extremely strong family loyalties and appreciation of their parents' sacrifices.

In reminiscing about the early homesteading days, Mary said that the greatest problems were: isolation, poor roads, lack of cash, and no electricity. Modern residents of the region have no idea of how hard it was for the early settlers – who helped build Alberta and Canada. One of Mary's weekly chores during the 1920s was to drive the wagon over the five rough miles to the railroad station at Sangudo to deliver the cream and pick up mail and supplies. The trip was an all-day job. A 5-gallon can of fresh cream then brought $1.00. No settlers yet lived along the trail to the village. The Lisses considered themselves lucky to live so close to the railroad. Their children went to the local one-room Poplar School until they went on to high school in Sangudo.

John Liss was extremely active in local politics and community services – so Mary accompanied him to meetings and conferences, and eventually became a popular officer in many community groups, including:
—The Royal Canadian Legion Auxilliary
—The Lac Ste Anne Historical Society
—The Historical Museum and the Women's Institute
She was a driving force in the publishing of the Lantern Era. Mary worked with John in the Co-op organizations and the C.C.F. and New Democratic Party. She was a member of:
—The Pembina Valley Old Timers
—The Sangudo Horticultural Club
—The George Pegg Gardens
—The Calf Club and 4-H Club
—Sangudo Home & School Association
—Sangudo Hobby Fair
—The Tri Psi Sorority
—The Canadian Girls in Training
—The United Church Ladies' Aid Society
—The Canadian Red Cross Society
—The Golden Age Club
—The Roydale Gay 67's

Mary canvassed for many organizations and willingly gave of her time for community events. She could be counted on.

Mary Liss – you were a grand lady. We are happy to have had the privilege of knowing and loving you.

A Nation is Born

1867   Canada Confederation
1905   Alberta province joins Dominion of Canada

John Liss Travels

June 23, 1892 (old style Julian calendar) born in Lithuania, part of White Russia. Moved to Radoszkowieze

July 10, 1892 Birthdate according to Gregorian calendar.

1903 John's father, Jan Pozarzyski emigrated to U.S.A.

1904 John, his mother and eight children emigrated to Toledo, Ohio.

1904 Attended public school in Toledo. Lived on farm in Freesoil, Michigan. Poor land.

1910 John worked as a printer, typesetter for a Polish newspaper. A book salesman of Polish books.

1910 Worked in a Milwaukee law office.

1910 Trip to Toronto Canadian National Exposition. 160 acres for $10 fee – Homestead Act.

1911 Set out for Winnipeg, Manitoba. Worked in British Columbia for David Gallatily. Picked fruit in B.C. Worked in Vernon, B.C. Went to Calgary, Alberta. Opened a book store. Sold real estate. Sold made-to-measure clothing.

1912 Visited Edmonton Land Office. Filed on land in Peace River. Filed on land in the Paddle River Valley. Did not perform their required homestead duties and forfeited their right to these parcels. Lost $10 filing fees on all the quarters.

1912 A major depression set in. Rampant unemployment. Returned to U.S. Worked in a copper mine in Montana. Visited Seattle looking for work.

1913 Joined U.S. Marine Corps because of promise of an education. Sent to Mazatlan, Mexico to await orders for invasion.

1913 – August 26 Mare Island, California received permission to change his name to John Liss #64067, 34 CO. 4th Regiment.

1914 – April 17 Honorable discharge from the U.S. Marines by purchase. Rank – Private. Character – excellent.

1914 Returned to Calgary. Operated bookstore with his father.

1916 Returned to Sangudo. Filed on homestead north of Sangudo. SE/ Quarter, section 24, Township 57, Range 7 West, 5th Meridian.

1917 Jan. 12 Joined Canadian Army. 253 Battalion Canada Expeditionary Force (#109263). 253 Queen's University Brigade, N.C.O. school, 2nd Polish Br. (Camp Borden, Niagara-on-the-Lake, Ontario). 2nd C.O.R.

1917 May Considered "very good, intelligent and would make a good officer" for the Polish Falcons. Promoted to Company Sergeant Major.

1917 – October 17 Legally changed his name to John Liss at the Supreme Court of Ontario in Toronto.

1917 Married Bernice Rynard in Ontario.

1918 Canadian Railway Troops, Paymaster Corps Purfleet, England. Sgt. Major.

1919 – Jan. 21 Discharge from C.E.F. at Toronto, Ontario. Conduct – very good. British War Medal.

1919 – Jan. 21 Son Kenneth Radimer Liss born in Toronto.

1919 Returned to Sangudo homestead to "prove-up" his land. Wife and son arrive later in year.

1920 – June 8 Bernice Liss died of tubercular spinal meningitis.

1921 Son Kenneth sent to relatives in Udora, Ontario.

1922 – Feb. 24 Married Mary Martha Fridel at Barrhead, Alberta.

1923 Son Stanley Francis born.

1925 Son Arthur Vlad born.

1927 Daughter Helen Veronica born.

1928 Farmhouse burns down.

1929 Son Edward born. Depression and low farm prices.

1931 Thadeus Ralph born.

1932 Charter Member of Canadian Legion.

1933 Valeria Aline Janine born.

1935 John Robert born. Social Credit Party sweeps into power in Alberta.

1935 Helped organize the United Farmers of Alberta and farm cooperatives.

1935 Telephones came into our area. Cable buried in 1972.

1938-1943 Operated Dominion Illustration Station.

1941 July 14   Enlisted in the Canadian Field Force at Edmonton. A/Sgt. #M65788. Served as recruiting officer in Edmonton and Calgary.

1943 – March 24 Medical discharge from the Canadian Army.

1950 "Got the power." Organized neighbors to supply poles and got rural electrification to our farm.

1953 Ran for political office as C.C.F. candidate (Cooperative Commonwealth Federation).

1957 Ran for political office as a C.C.F. candidate.

1958 Zone Commander Royal Canadian Legion.

1963 Ran for office as New Democratic candidate.

Lifetime Achievements

Farm Advisor to Alexis Indian Reserve
Elimination of fishing license fees for seniors
Queen's Golden Jubilee Medal
Centennial Medal of Canada
Meritorious Service Medal
Zone Commander of Canadian Legion
British War Medal

Memoirs on file at Glenbow Museum, Calgary, Alberta, Canada

THE SENATE

CANADA

O t t a w a,
K1A 0A4

July 25, 1972.

Mrs. L. F. Ivanhoe,
Apt. 36,
5301 Demaret,
Bakersfield, Cal.
93309

Dear Mrs. Ivanhoe:

Thank you for your letter of July 14th which was on my desk when I returned from England tonight, after spending two delightful weeks at an International Affairs Conference in Sussex.

I was delighted to be able to join the rest of you in honouring your parents who have made a great contribution to the development of Alberta. As a matter of fact, I think the story of their work and success should be written up because it's the story of a pioneer immigrant coming to Canada with nothing but his strength and determination and the result is he has made good in a large way. The success of the whole family is a tribute to everyone concerned.

With kindest regards and every good wish, I am

Yours sincerely,

Donald Cameron.

Dictated on July 24th.

Senator Donald Cameron pays tribute to his friends, John and Mary Liss

ISBN 142510431-2

9 781425 104313